Where Does the Wild Goose Go?

Where Does the Wild Goose Go?

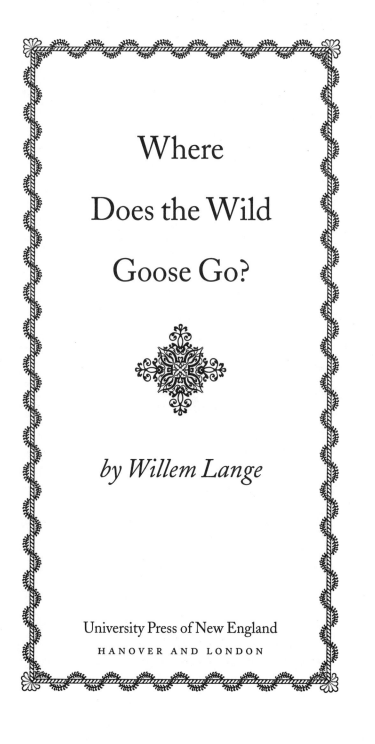

by Willem Lange

University Press of New England

HANOVER AND LONDON

University Press of New England, Hanover, NH 03755

© 2002 by Willem Lange

Printed in the United States of America

5   4   3   2   1

LIBRARY OF CONGRESS CATALOGING-IN-PUBLICATION DATA

Lange, Willem, 1935–
    Where does the wild goose go? / by Willem Lange.
        p.   cm.
    "Most of the stories in this collection have appeared in edited form in
The Valley News, Lebanon, New Hampshire. Some of them have also been
aired by the author on Vermont Public Radio as part of his regular commentary"—T.p. verso.
    ISBN 1–58465–190–3 (pbk.   :   alk. paper)
    1. Lange, Willem, 1935–   —Friends and associates.
2. Lange, Willem, 1935–   —Anecdotes.
3. United States—Social life and customs — Anecdotes.   I. Title.
CT275.L2723 A3   2002
973.9'092—dc21   2001004981

Most of the stories in this collection have appeared in edited form in *The
Valley News,* Lebanon, New Hampshire. Some of them have also been aired
by the author on Vermont Public Radio as part of his regular commentary
series.

TO *Ida*

THE NEVER-ENDING SOURCE

OF A MILLION BRIGHT IDEAS

Life is rather like opening a tin of sardines:
We're all of us looking for the key.

—*Beyond the Fringe*

How does it come about that certain souls can never find peace, either on the heights, on the surface of the earth, or in the depths of the ocean?

—*Halldór Laxness*

Contents

Where Does the Wild Goose Go?

Looking for God

I'M NOT ENTIRELY SURE THIS IS TRUE, but probably one of the best things my family ever did for me as a child was imbue me with the conviction that there was a God. At the same time, one of the worst things they did was assure me there was no need for me to ponder or question what His essence might be; that it already had been revealed; that all I had to do was "accept" Him. My grandfather was a Gideon, one of those devout evangelicals who anonymously supply hotel rooms and homeless shelters with Bibles. I don't know how many little pocket testaments he gave me over the years, in which I dutifully filled in the printed statement on the flyleaf, attesting that I had once again accepted Christ as my personal savior.

All that was perfectly lovely, I suppose. Christ seemed like a splendid and very helpful person to have as a friend. The only fly in the ointment was that, though he was said to love me, he was also purported to know my every thought. I was an imaginative child—still am, as a matter of fact—and those two facts, side by side, did not bring my heart ease. Quite early I decided there was little chance of pleasing him with my inmost thoughts and impulses. Instead, I began a lifetime of vaguely hoping I'd know when my end was near and further opportunities for sinning were unlikely to occur, so that, like the thief Dismas at Golgotha, I could pull my fat from the fire at the last possible moment and enter Paradise through grace, unscathed and unsinged.

Years went by, and other dissonance crept into my consciousness. It became likely that the world had not been created in six days. It became clear that Galileo had been right, and the clerics wrong who threatened him with burning at the stake as a heretic. It became evident that the most disagreeable people in the world were those who were certain they had the answers, argued from questionable authority to prove it, and predicted the confusion of those who disagreed. Finally it became impossible for me to imagine that Heaven was a pleasant place to be, if all those who were pretty sure they were going there, were. Like Huckleberry Finn, I made up my mind I wouldn't try for it; and like him, I didn't say so, because it would only make trouble and do no good. So to this day I suffer cramps in my smiling muscles after hours of enduring the need, for social reasons, to appear to agree with the most egregious and nonsensical preaching from the Word of God.

Still, that early-planted seed has grown into a persistent weed of longing and wondering: Is the numinous accessible? Is there a way to break through the membrane that seems to separate this life from any other? The way, for example, that John Magee describes in his famous poem "High Flight." And if there is, can my thoroughly Western consciousness tear itself away from its mundane preoccupations long enough to achieve it?

I have always doubted it. Though advancing age has brought me ever closer to the moment when I shall discover everything, or nothing, that doubt has not diminished. And yet, over the past sixty and more years, there have been incidents—half a dozen, perhaps—during which I sensed a translucence in the membrane and viewed, as through a mist or a sheet of ice, moving figures in an irresistible but inscrutable scenario that always just eluded my understanding. Like the little crippled boy of Hamelin, left behind when the Pied Piper led all his friends into the mountain, I have been left sadly wondering what delights others may have attained. Nowadays I wonder no longer—or at least I no longer chase those phantoms. I can wait till we meet on an equal footing.

When I leave my home for more than a few days, I usually carry a journal with me. There's one beside me here on the desk right now. It's a little brown spiral notebook, quite a bit the worse for wear and wrinkled by frequent wettings. Its front cover has fallen off, so I keep it in a little plastic zip-top bag. In it are recorded some of the best days of my life.

Monday, July 31, 1995—7:45 P.M.—More of those lousy headwinds! They blew all day long, and the puffs could almost stop you dead. Rapids most of the day, too— pretty bony, most of 'em. Ran most, lined some, carried one. Ernst and Ed hit a rock, filled, and got dumped out. Got pretty wet and cold, changing clothes in the sleet; but they managed to get a little drier and carried on. Finally ran the last rapid before tidewater and camped in a sheltered spot about 10 kilometers from the outer river mouth.

If this wind keeps up, I don't know how we're ever going to get there.

On that last day of July, six of us in three canoes had just reached the mouth of a lovely little river flowing into Bathurst Inlet, above the Arctic Circle on the north coast of Canada. Hiukitak River, it was called in Inuktitut, meaning "place of beautiful sand." But we'd seen precious little sand during the previous two weeks. The hills on both sides of the river were bare, scoured, black basalt, heavy and gloomy in cold, gray weather, but enlivened every so often by the distant white dots of arctic wolves, wagging their tails and keeping pace with us as we paddled through their territories. Now finally, at the mouth, we discovered the reason for the river's name, and remembered that most rivers in the far North were named in antiquity by native people who usually did not follow them upstream during the summer.

For me, one of the charms of outdoor life is the unpredictability of its conditions. A river, for example, may be too high, too low, or just right; the wind ahead or behind or still; the weather wet, dry, cold or hot. It's in our reactions to these conditions that we discover our essential qualities. Those of us accustomed to being in control, or perhaps needing to be, often become anxious when events fail to accord with our well-laid plans. We always see most clearly into our own souls—and the souls of others, too—when adversity has peeled us, like onions, several layers deep.

Until we reached the mouth of the river, our trip in 1995 had gone pretty much as planned. A charter

4

plane on floats had dropped us off at the headwater lake of the river, and we had made our way slowly downstream through country virtually unmarked by our own species. By some of the best fishing holes, always at the foot of the first rapid after a lake, we found Inuit tent rings—circles of stones that once had held down the edges of caribou-skin tents. Twice, on the bare summits of hills beside our own camps, we came across much smaller, oval rings of stones. The local Inuit, who called themselves *Krangmiut,* the People Beyond, could not possibly bury their dead in solid rock or earth frozen hard as steel. Instead, they carried them to nearby hilltops and left them there in their sleeping bags, surrounded by the ovals of stones. Scavengers made short work of the remains; and the stones kept the spirits from wandering restlessly until a new creature—it could be a baby or a puppy—was born to the band and named after the person left on the hilltop. Then the spirit was at peace.

One day, in a small thicket of head-high willows halfway across a portage, we did come across the remains of a long-ago trapper's winter camp—rusty pieces of a sheet-steel stove, a few empty tomato cans from a Hudson's Bay trading post, and an old tobacco tin. Except for that, and the rings of stone, nothing.

There was a time, not too long ago, when the Inuit frequented this valley during the winter. Summertimes, they stayed near the coast, fishing and sealing. But after the freeze-up and the first snow, they traveled by dog team in their never-ending search for game or inland lakes where they might jig through the ice for the lake trout, long as a man's arm, that live in almost all of them.

With Otokreak's dog team leading, we left the Burnside mission early next morning in the gloomy polar night. Although clouds covered the sky, it was bitterly cold. Within half an hour we skirted small Koagiuk Island at the entrance of Bathurst Harbor and at noon crossed the solidly frozen Bathurst Inlet, only five miles wide at this point. We then headed for Gordon Bay or Hiorkretak, meaning "a nice sandy beach." That night we made camp in an abandoned igloo in the Umingmaktok foothills, named for the musk oxen hunted there.

We spent the entire next day in a slow, tiring climb between gentle slopes of sedimentary and terrace-like trap rocks to reach the plateau, where my combination barometer-altimeter showed an elevation of 1050 feet. Looking south, back towards Gordon Bay, we faced a desolation of countless hills eroded by time. Nevertheless, I felt elated because, as I knew, I was the first White Man to explore this land!

That's a description of the river in 1938, fifty-seven years before our group reached the same spot. The writer was Raymond de Coccola, a native of Corsica and an Oblate missionary among the Inuit of the north coast of Canada. He writes of the first days of his first extended winter trip, and his first view of the Hiukitak. (His spelling is different from that of the current maps, and his pronunciation different from that of contemporary Inuktitut; any attempt at rendering Inuktitut in English is bound to suffer from differences in local dialects. Inuktitut was not a written language until the missionaries began devising ways to render it.)

Father de Coccola—the Inuit nicknamed him "Little Man," or simply called him "Fala," the closest they could come easily to "Father"—was an amazing human being who observed keenly, accepted his new friends' values, beliefs, and idiosyncrasies without judgment, healed the sick as well as he could with the few medicines he carried, and witnessed to his faith only when asked a direct question. Like, "Why would a smart person like you, Fala, come from a home where it is warm all the time to a place like this?" Father de Coccola spent twelve years among the Inuit and was invalided out in 1949, at the age of thirty-seven. His book, *The Incredible Eskimo*, was first published in 1956 as *Ayorama*—Inuktitut for "It can't be helped; that's life." I discovered it three years after our own trip.

Wednesday, August 2, 1995—Made 7 kilometers yesterday, fighting incoming tide, rain, and really bad headwinds. Stopped at the last possible shelter, a steep river bank on the north shore, and made camp on a narrow beach just above high tide line. There were huge combers out in Bathurst Inlet; we weren't going anywhere. Settled down to wait. Checked the wind several times during the night. No change. Depressing—mainly because a couple of the guys are getting anxious about our rendezvous with the pickup schooner. They keep asking questions that begin, "Well, what if . . .?" and end, ". . . what'll we do then?" We're supposed to be there by tomorrow night, and we've got about twenty miles of salt water to cross.

I had arranged with the captain of an elderly forty-seven-foot schooner, the *MV Fort Hearne*, to meet us on August 3rd at or near Burnside Village on the west side of Bathurst Inlet. But here on the east shore, the north wind seemed to blow harder with each hour. Tucked beneath our hillside beside the estuary, we hunkered in our tents reading, searched for firewood and fresh water, and poked through abandoned Inuit campsites along the shore. Eric found a rotting wooden jolly boat, and Ed dug up a waterlogged Anglican prayer book transcribed into Inuktitut. Beyond poking around or bringing our journals up to date, there wasn't much else to do except swap books with each other and scan the bay with the binoculars. The breaking waves out in the channel were about eight feet high. I wasn't as concerned as some of the others that the schooner would leave the inlet without us. The captain, Larry Whittaker, was a good friend and an old Arctic hand. I knew that if we failed to arrive at the rendezvous, he'd come looking for us along our probable course.

All day long I stewed, while the anxiety level around me intensified. Finally I couldn't take the useless speculation anymore. Right behind camp, facing the ocean, stood a magnificent basalt crag, about seven hundred feet high and shaped like Cape Horn. If ever there was a spot in which to commune with the spirits that animated this place, that hill was it. The Inuit, untouched by alien influences for millennia in their arctic isolation, could see the supernatural virtually everywhere. And that huge, glacier-scoured rock looked to me like one of their particular spirit places.

Glances into the indefinite past by old people like Itireitok and Manerathiak provided fantastic notions about their world. For them . . . the land is inhabited by supernatural beings. Some of them are good and harmless—souls of the dead who roam the land to help until they come to their final rest in a place of happiness called Heaven. They always protect the tired and sick against evil spirits and ghouls. The ghouls delight in misleading the unwary traveler during stormy weather and causing distress.

"They are around all the time," Itireitok assured me. "We call them 'Tupilain.' They may be shy or fiendish. They are always breathing and whispering, like the wind itself. Sometimes they look like men. Sometimes like animals or mysterious hybrids. Raised out of nowhere, like the hills and mountains, the rivers, lakes, and seas."

. . . Itireitok used the same word 'anernek' to denote breath, soul, and spirit, because her own soul was living and breathing, capable of survival after death. Without knowing it, she was explaining her belief in animism, the doctrine that natural phenomena, animal life, and inanimate objects have souls. (Father de Coccola, *The Incredible Eskimo*, 80)

"I'm going up the hill," I announced, "and talk to the author of this weather. Anybody want to come?" Nobody stirred.

I felt a little like Moses going up that mountain. The wind was strong enough to lean on. After a while I reached a grassy col dividing the peak from the bleak hills behind it. On each side of the cleft stood a line of *inuksuks,* human-shaped cairns of rock, arms sticking straight out from the shoulders beneath their boulder heads, built there to funnel south-migrating caribou through the pass and down to the river below, where the hunters would kill as many as they could against the long starvation of winter. It was a perfect spot for an ambush, as well as a perfect spot to commune with whatever spirit had inspired this weather. But suddenly, as I thought of the people who had survived here for so many centuries—responding stoically to fortune good and bad, starvation and plenty, and playing their never-ending cat-and-mouse game with death—my concerns seemed laughable, and the anxieties of my friends embarrassing, before whatever spirit lived in this wind.

I spoke to it. "Look," I said, "I came up here to talk to you about this weather. But that's stupid. All I'd really like is to have a glimpse of your face."

I meant it as much as anything I had ever said; but nothing happened. I waited a few minutes and, beginning to shiver, started down. Just then, something caught my eye. Deep in a crack in the rocks at the base of a black cliff, where a freezing person might huddle for shelter from the wind, lay a human skull and pelvis. Someone else long ago had come up here to the cliffs seeking something beyond.

A few hours later the wind began to diminish. By morning it was safe to start. By midnight we'd made our long crossing and were waiting for the schooner. Three years later, in de Coccola's book, I found a hint about the bones of the other seeker on the hilltop.

"What happened to Manerathiak, Nokadlak?"
"Who knows? We had pitched our tents at the mouth of

the Hiorkretak River. It was a rainy, windy morning. Old Manerathiak walked along the shore towards the cliffs overlooking the bay. She did not come back."

"And you don't know where she went?"

Everyone stared at me in astonishment. Nokadlak chuckled, "She went to the top of the highest cliff facing the sea. The weather was stormy. The waves angry and high. She simply disappeared, Fala."

Cato Passes

I CHECKED CATO'S BOWLS IN THE morning. There was still plenty of water in one, but he was down to about two tablespoonfuls of food. So I put cat food on my shopping list and when I stopped for groceries about noon, picked up a fresh bag. But when I went to pour the fresh food into the bowl at mid-afternoon, he still hadn't touched the last of the old. Same with the water. Hmm. That wasn't routine. I wondered where he was.

He'd been with us twelve years; he came the same year I built my last house. I had a young fellow helping me. He'd just gotten married and had given his bride a little white kitten. But the kitten had a bad habit. "He sucks lace!" he told me, obviously offended. "Whenever Kim sits down or lies down in her nightgown, he jumps up and starts sucking on the lace on the front. It grosses her out, so I've got to get rid of him."

Sure enough, he did suck lace. Kneaded it with his front paws, too, and purred and drooled at the same time. Probably he'd been taken away from his mother too young. But we've always had soft spots in our hearts for little creatures damaged in infancy—and we could use a good mouser—so Cato became a part of our family.

He got his name because, like the inimitable Inspector Clouseau's valet, Cato, he lurked in hiding when I came home, and leaped at me with a sudden, tigerlike rush. I played with him the same game that Clouseau played—"I know you are here, you little devil!"—and sneaked silently through the quiet rooms, ready to be terrified. Cats, though, can't seem to quiet the nervous twitching of their tails when they're about to pounce. Often as not, I'd see his tail sticking up from behind the arm of the sofa or the coffee table, and we'd pounce at each other.

He also had the irritating habit of silently trailing anyone entering a room that was usually closed and unheated. So the first thing to do, whenever he was missing, was to go through the house, opening the doors to the attic, cellar, guest room, and all the closets. When you got the right door, there he was, waiting, with a little bubble of a meow. Off he went to his food dish, and thence to the front door, to be let out.

This time, though, nothing. I even found myself opening kitchen cabinet doors and peeking into places he'd never been in the twelve years I'd known him. I went through the garage and up the ladder to the loft, where he often spent winter nights. Nothing. I walked around the house, tchking with my tongue against my teeth. At this time of the year, just after the snow is gone, a snow-white cat is the easiest thing in the world to see . . . if he's there. I spotted half a dozen chunks of birch bark blown down by the winter wind, a fragment of a paper towel, and one of Mother's little garden angels. But no Cato.

I went inside. "Have you seen the cat today?" I asked. Mother's suggestions didn't plow any new ground. But I couldn't sit still. Stupidly I retraced all the possibilities I'd just exhausted.

The noose of an inevitable conclusion was tightening around the neck of all the optimistic scenarios I could devise. This had happened to us before. In the cases of the cats, we rarely found the corpses; but I've buried more than my share of pets, and found it a bitter job: the quiet body lying beyond the growing hole; the family looking tearfully out the windows; the laying in the ground; the regretful farewell and quick covering up; and sitting at last beside the fresh-turned earth, tasting metallic grief at the mandible joint.

That night, just before bed and after a dozen trips out onto the porch, I had to look once more. I took the big flashlight in a circuit through the nearest woods and was startled again by the same bits of birch bark. No cat. And none the next morning, when the dog and I went down for the paper. It had been a cold night. "Why don't you look by daylight?" Mother asked.

Living on the edge of the woods as we do, we're also on the edge of other creatures' territories. The deer feed on our neighbors' rhododendrons; bears in the spring tear down the bird feeders; owls hoot from the swamp; and the cries of coyotes echo around the hillsides in the quiet nights. The woods are peaceful and serene, but they're also teeming with unseen predators, from shrews to fishers and foxes. Nor was Cato a completely innocent little white house kitty. Many the morning, on my way out for the paper, that I almost stepped on one of his grisly little offerings.

Calling the dog, I started a big clockwise circle

about seventy-five yards in radius, around the house. I could see just about everything between me and the yard. I moved slowly, as if hunting, taking in the new view every three steps. The dog cruised around me, glancing at me about every dozen steps, as she always does. She knows far more than I do what's going on around us. With sudden inspiration, I asked, "Where's the kitty cat?"

She walked away, and I continued circling. She came back, and suddenly I remembered the odd way she tracks things for me: continuing only as long as I show interest. So I walked in the direction from which she had just come.

I spotted him from thirty yards away, a blob of white fur against the brown needles and duff beneath a hemlock tree. There was no point in getting there in a hurry, but I couldn't help it. There was fur scattered in a six-foot circle; brown oak leaves were spattered with blood. He'd been killed and half-eaten, from the head rearward, his skin peeled back as if by a human hunter. I lifted his body and turned him over, trying to recreate the scene of his death, hoping it had been quick and without terror, but doubting it. The dog sat a few feet away, incurious, scanning the woods like the little secret service agent that she is.

I dug the hole and laid in it what was left of Cato; scratched one last time the spot on his spine just ahead of his tail; smoothed his fur—so long, buddy—and filled the hole. I carried two stones from the wall nearby and covered him against being dug up. Then I had to go tell Mother.

His bowls are gone from the laundry, and after the cleaning lady comes tomorrow, the last of his hair will be gone from the living room furniture. The little soprano snore is gone from under the bed. I can sit and read without having my book pushed aside. Like a stream flowing around a rock, our lives have begun to close again, and it almost seems as if Cato never existed. But if he never had, there wouldn't now be this hole where he used to be, for almost a fifth of my life. Soon, I hope, the delightful pleasure of what he was will efface the pain of his leaving.

Adventures of a YMCA Boy

EVEN AFTER MORE THAN FIFTY YEARS, it takes very little to bring it all back. A dish of tapioca pudding—fish eyes and glue—will do it. A puff of wind blowing from a grove of white pines on a hot day. Rings of brown dirt around my ankles under my socks after walking a dusty trail. The reek of a wet towel thrown into a corner and forgotten. Any of these sensations will do it: will recall the creaking, rocking school bus full of young boys chugging north on old Route 11 from Syracuse to Watertown, then over dusty county roads, and finally arriving, to a soprano cheer from everybody aboard, at an inverted triangle perched atop a rustic portal of spruce poles from which hung a row of letters wrought from white birch twigs—YMCA CAMP TOUSEY.

It's happened to a lot of us, and left indelible impressions. Of course it has; it's a dress rehearsal for ten-year-olds of what's going to happen to them about eight years later, when their urge to leave their parents' nest will be as great as their parents' desire for them to leave, and soon. On a particular summer Sunday afternoon our mothers and fathers took us downtown to meet the camp bus. We wore brand-new sneakers and shorts. Pinned inside the breast pocket of our shirts were two one-dollar bills to be

deposited in the camp bank for candy and crafts sup-
plies. Dragging at the end of one arm was an impos-
sibly heavy war-surplus duffel bag. And dragging
already at our hearts were the first pangs of loneliness
and homesickness.

If kids instead of parents were allowed to make the
decision, summer camps would all be out of business
within five years, because no kid would want to go
for the first time. What a trauma! Especially when
you know that everything about you—your spectacles, your haircut, your clothes, your pink knees and
skinny arms, even your name—everything about you
looks or sounds stupid. But kids don't get to make
the final decisions, so there you are.

YMCA—Young Men's Christian Association.
How very old that sounds now, when we've all
become so self-conscious. Our Christianity then was
understated, understood, and implicit; our grace
before meals and benedictions at evening were clearly from an evangelical tradition. But my cabin mates,
one year that I remember, included kids like Pat
McGarrity, David Goldberg, and Fenimore Cooper.
Nobody made waves or seemed to notice. We were
there to go to camp.

How is it possible that we ever could have enjoyed
it enough to want to go back another year? And yet
we did. For after that first shocking day when everything was new and disorienting, and we knew no one
else, the rituals carried us through. There were
morning colors, breakfast, cabin inspection, activity
periods, lunch, afternoon nap . . . There was mail
call, with its letters and packages from home, full of
cookies and clean socks. And there were for each of

us one or two favorite staff members who could be trusted—who reached out to us through the confusion and our own ineptitude, and smiled, and tried to help. They taught us archery and riflery, boondoggling, swimming, orienteering, Morse Code, and dozens of new songs. The excitement of learning and doing new stuff pushed the self-consciousness into the background. It was only during quiet periods, or the wakeful minutes before sleep came each night, that the homesickness tried to return.

The only knots I had ever tied in my life before I went to Camp Tousey were the ones in my shoes and the ones around bundles of newspapers. But just outside the mess hall there was a knot board with pieces of rope hanging down, where our cabin counselor taught us a new knot each day. To the one of us who could tie the most knots the fastest (nobody could win twice; former winners coached those who hadn't won yet) he gave his dessert each night. At the time, I suppose it didn't occur to any of us that he might have liked the dessert himself. We all learned them all—faithful square knot and despised granny, sheet bend, bowline ("The rabbit comes out of the hole, goes around the tree . . ."), clove hitch, sheepshank, carrick bend, the whole board. I've never forgotten even one of them, or him. They've been companions of mine for over five decades, though his is the only name I've forgotten.

The lake had the strongest attraction for me. Not swimming; boats and fishing. The camp owned a fleet of clunky sheet-steel rowboats and several wood-and-canvas canoes. To qualify to take out rowboats during free period, we had to pass a one-hundred-yard swimming test down at the beach area. If we wanted to take out a canoe, the test was lengthened: from the boathouse to Royal Island, a wooded, crown-shaped island a quarter of a mile from the boathouse. I was a side-stroker and had difficulty seeing where I was going. I knew I'd made it when I saw the trees of the island out of the corner of my eye, towering above me. What I didn't know at the time was how many years, and how many thousands of miles, I would spend in canoes from that moment on. As I sit here in my office in March, fifty-five years later, typing these words, there are paintings and prints of canoes and small boats all around me, on every wall; on a table beside me the plans for this summer's trip to the Arctic; and out in a shed attached to the side of my house, a rack of lovely old canoes waiting for spring.

A young junior camp counselor with the improbable name of Graham Cubberly wanted more than anything else to start a sailing program. The camp had just received from a friend of the YMCA a donation of an old wooden catboat. It lay upside down in the poison ivy–haunted woods beyond the volleyball court, uncaulked, unpainted, and about to start rotting. For two weeks, four hours a day, Graham and several of us fellow sailors-to-be (who at home had to be forced to mow the lawn) scraped, sanded, caulked, and painted. Two days before the end of camp, we finally launched our resurrection, stepped the mast, tightened the shrouds and stay, and raised the sail. We made it about fifty yards from the dock before a strong puff of wind caught us. With Graham screaming, "Let go of the rope! Let go of the rope!" we slowly, grandly, ignominiously toppled over. The Camp Director had been watching. Frightened half to death by the episode, he banned further sailing that camp session. But what a glorious fifty yards!

The mess hall service was composed of random seconds from Syracuse China, and ran heavily to Knights of Columbus plates and St. Francis of Assisi bowls. The beverage of choice was cherry or raspberry bug juice, which left our tongues and lips bright red. The entree was usually war-surplus mystery meat in a pan of macaroni and cheese. Waiting for dessert, we sang "Here We Sit Like Birds in the Wilderness" or the interminable "This Is Table Number One." One counselor was famous for playing and singing "Freight Train Blues," and one wispy, whimsical camper for performing a heart-rending a capella version of "Old Shep." The drug of choice in those days was not what you might think, but Kaopectate—especially after the hot water heater in the kitchen went on the fritz for several days. And the most popular evening program occurred the last night of camp: an evening of skits, campers' awards, snipe hunts, and the valedictory speech from the Director at what was called—in deference to the Iroquois who had inhabited the forest before we Europeans arrived—the Council Fire.

After the goofy skits had ended and the awards had been given and applauded, the great fire began to die down, and the occasion turned serious. The Director invariably ended his speech with the benediction, "The Lord watch between me and thee while we are absent one from the other." A long silence followed, broken only by the rustlings of the dying fire and the croaking of bullfrogs along the shore. Then, "Thanks, fellows. 'Taps' in twenty minutes. See you in the morning."

But one year we had a genuine Iroquois junior counselor, an Onondaga named Lloyd Elm. Biddy, as he was called, had been teaching a crafts group to make Indian costumes and perform native dances for different occasions. As an added attraction on the last night of camp, he and his group were going to do a ritual dance invoking the Great Spirit. It was going to be a real production number. They built an altar of rocks in shallow water—the bottom there was pretty mucky, so it took a lot of rocks—about thirty feet offshore, and laid the council fire on top of that. Just in front of it they built several little underwater pyramids of rock and, floating a long section of discarded wooden dock over to the site, set it on the pyramids so that it made a platform right at water level. (At least it was at water level when they built it.) The plan was that at the height of the most serious part of the ceremonies that evening, they would emerge from the darkness and do their Great Spirit dance, seeming from the shore to be virtually dancing on the water.

The night was black as tar, with a new moon and thousands of stars. The Director, after giving out the Outstanding Camper awards, held up his hand conspicuously for silence. From out on the dark lake came the faint, distant throb of a tom-tom. We sat entranced upon the bank. Closer and closer came the heartlike beating, till out of the night and into the glare of the bonfire glided the camp war canoe, newly decorated with mystic symbols and carrying Biddy and eight or ten of his painted braves. Silently, solemnly they climbed out of the canoe and arranged themselves on the platform. The tom-tom player stood at one end, the rest in two parallel lines facing each other in pairs. The drum beat began to intensify.

If you've ever seen an Indian dance, you're familiar with one common step: The dancer slides the ball of his foot forward, dragging it on the ground, and then stamps down with that heel. At the same time he bends forward and does a sort of uppercut with first one fist and then the other. Biddy and his braves began to do this in unison, chanting in rhythm with the drum.

Poor souls! They'd rehearsed for weeks out by the horseshoe pits, but they'd never tried it on that chunk of old dock. The rocks supporting it had sunk a little under their weight. Every time they stamped down with their heels in unison and bent over, lake water squirted up between the boards and hit them right in the face. Those old boards were right at water level and about as flexible as rubber. It looked as though they were stepping on a colony of clams. At first we were horrified. But then someone began to titter, and within moments the whole audience, over a hundred of us, were convulsed, rolling on the ground or helplessly down the bank into the water. Water and paint were running off the dancers in streams. But half-drowned as they were, they danced on, though the tom-tom player was reduced almost to paralysis.

At the climax of the dance, Biddy shouted, "Ho!" and the tom-tom stopped abruptly. In the surprising silence that followed, broken now only by faint paroxysms from the shore, he raised his arms and prepared to give the benediction in Iroquois. He took a deep breath and began, "O Gitchee Mani . . . O Gitchee Manito . . ." His shoulders heaved suddenly. "O Jeez!" he cried, turned abruptly around and dove off the dock into the lake. But he'd forgotten the water was only about a foot deep there and the bottom very muddy. It was like a cartoon. Biddy's legs waved frantically in the air, silhouetted against the fire, as he struggled to back out of the muck. Finally two of his braves jumped in after him, and the Director mercifully, sonorously pulled the curtain on the whole wonderful, unforgettable scene.

So it was that my annual exile wasn't without its compensations. I've often, in fact, wished to return to those scenes of boyhood. But they tell me it's impossible. The YMCA has sold the lakeside land to a developer, and I wouldn't want to see it now. I do hope that Biddy, if he's still alive, won't take it amiss if I'm never able to catch a whiff of cherry Kool-Aid or a moldy bathing suit without thinking of him, his braves, and the Great Spirit. I hope to see them all again someday.

Objects Infused with Life

Every object rightly seen unlocks a quality of the soul.
—RALPH WALDO EMERSON

I'D LIKE TO MEET THE MAN WHO HUNG the head on my wood-splitting maul, because he did a beautiful job. The head hangs just right, with its chin tucked in ever so slightly; and he used a wooden wedge to hold it. Thus, when it loosened, as big hammerheads always do after a year or so, I was able to tighten it up easily with small metal hammer wedges driven crosswise. Someday, of course, my mind will wander while I'm using the maul. I'll get careless for just a moment, overshoot the splitting wedge, and snap the handle. But in the meantime, I never take the maul out of the shed and head for the woodpile without hefting it once or twice and sharing a silent moment with that anonymous Stradivari of the splitting maul factory.

My wife and I sit at opposite ends of the dinner table in my great-grandmothers' chairs. My wife sits in Great-Grandma Walther's cherrywood armchair, an expression of Victorian sensibility. But not, alas, of good craftsmanship. The joints are all loose, and the chair's design aggravates the condition. Its maker did not sign his name to it. I sit in Great-Grandma Lange's rush-bottom armchair, as sound as the day over a hundred years ago that somebody named F. A. Sinclair of Plottsville, New York, stamped his name and home town into one of its hard maple back slats and shipped it out of his shop.

Objects. They're everywhere around us, almost unnoticed because they're so familiar a part of our lives. But they express our nature and our personal history more clearly and indelibly than anything we might say or write. Those of us who have sorted through a deceased person's effects can remember how the essence of the decedent was expressed by his possessions—and how their value bore no relation to what they might bring at auction.

I have beside me here on my desk an inexpensive silver-plated pocket watch that my wife gave me the day I finally graduated from college. Its price even then was not great; either of us could earn it now in less than two hours. The silver plating of the case has worn partly off, and the face has discolored. But on that long-ago day it represented for my wife an entire year of scrimping, and it is dearer to me than if it were of solid platinum and studded with diamonds.

Every object rightly seen . . . says Emerson. I'm not sure I quite agree with him. I'm not sure he would himself, if he could see a battery-operated toilet seat that makes a rude noise when someone sits on it, or a nativity set cast in milk chocolate. It's only in an object that is the serious, honest expression of its creator's spirit, or which by long use and familiarity has become a part of us, that we find the key unlocking our deepest responses. Then it's like opening a cedar closet that's been closed for the summer months against the moths: what a wealth of associations flows out into the room with that aroma!

Rummaging around in the attic the other day, I came across an old, olive-drab metal box: a World War II ammunition box. It had been a part of that great, irresistible flood of semi-useful war-surplus equipment that swept the country between 1945 and 1955. It was my first fishing equipment box. I'd thought it lost years ago. I brought it back down to the kitchen and opened it.

There was a smell of stale metal and rust and must. An old Prince Albert tobacco can held an assortment of snelled fishhooks, some still threaded with the mummified remains of ancient night crawlers. There was one of my mother's Bakelite-handled kitchen knives with silvery fish scales still stuck to the blade. It's too late now by decades ever to give it back to her. The bottom of the box was a mess of rusty, chipped spoons, spinners, and wooden plugs. In the corner lay my first trout-fishing reel, with the line still on it. When I pulled out the line, it crumbled into ashes. But the reel still clicked, with that familiar sound I'd recognize at midnight in the Gobi Desert. The handle was bent where I'd stepped on it once, and bits of sand still clung in the slots of the screws.

A dollar forty-nine it had cost me, brand-new; and I'd like a dollar for every six-inch trout it reeled in from the limestone brooks of central New York, for every swamp and rainstorm we sloshed through, for every time we came home together hours late and were exiled from each other for the following week. I carried it out onto the back porch, took it apart, cleaned and oiled it. Afterward my hands smelled of verdigris and sewing machine oil.

There was still more in the box: an oil-stained manila envelope with a couple of books. First was the *Handbook for Boys,* the Boy Scout manual, 1945 edition, with a Norman Rockwell cover, fifty cents. Harry Truman and Herbert Hoover, respectively, were listed as Honorary President and Vice-President. Then there was a book of familiar hymns, *Soul Stirring Songs,* with old favorites like "I've Pitched my Tent in Beulah" and "Let the Lower Lights Be Burning." Riffling through the handbook, I found a photograph used as a bookmark at page 270, "Nature in Waterways." It was an old-style narrow rectangular photo, taken with a Kodak Brownie box camera, of a plumpish kid in spectacles holding a bait-casting rod in one hand and a pretty good-sized smallmouth in the other. He's wearing baggy Navy surplus blue jeans, a flannel shirt out at the tail, and a pair of dark-blue, high-cut sneakers with the little white rubber circles at the shins. Talk about cedar closets and verdigris! I can still smell those sneakers!

I was sort of browsing through all this, remembering and trying to decide what to do with it, when my younger daughter came into the room. The youngest of our children, she's the only one of them in whom the vagrant genetic enthusiasm for fishing seems to have emerged. She looked at the stuff on the kitchen counter. "Hey," she said, "that reminds me. You haven't taken me fishing yet this year."

So the next day, a Sunday afternoon of warm sunshine and a soft north breeze, we biked over to a neighbor's pond. The trout were strong and hungry, and with the little spinning rod she caught at least twice as many as I. Her delighted laughter bubbled like music over the water as the rod throbbed in her hands. Shaking the fish off the barbless hooks as they came to her, she knelt gazing into the water as each slid back down the submarine slope of the dam and out of sight.

After a while she asked to try the fly rod. I handed it to her. "Gosh! Where'd you get this old reel?" she asked.

I told her. She turned it over, reading the label. Freshly oiled and polished, it was no bigger around than an old-fashioned silver dollar. "Gee, can I have this someday?" she asked. "You know, when you . . . uh, when you're done with it?" She stopped, embarrassed, and I thought of my mother's long-lost kitchen knife.

"It's yours," I answered, quite touched. So there in the warm Sunday afternoon sun on the bank of the pond, we traded objects that had unlocked the quality of our souls. I gave her the promise of an old brass fishing reel someday after I've caught my last trout. She gave me the imperishable gift of a young girl's laughter over the water.

Oradour-sur-Glane

On a lazy early summer afternoon—June 10, 1944—the little farming village of Oradour-sur-Glane hummed quietly in the sun. The trolley car that ran occasionally up and down the main street stood by its barn at the upper end of town. At the foot, the River Glane flowed clear and cold under sheltering willows past the old limestone mill. A boy playing hooky from school fished for trout along its banks. The smell of fresh-cut hay hung in the air.

Up at the Renault garage, a mechanic swore over a balky bolt; old-timers sat on the bench in front of the pharmacy; the whirr of a sewing machine drifted through the window of the dressmaker's shop; and the sound of kids' voices floated from the boys' and girls' schools.

Today, like that one, is also a sunny day, but with the chill of late winter still in the air. Mother and I are driving north from Limoges toward the Loire Valley. She was browsing through the guide book a couple of hours ago, and happened across the story of Oradour. It's not much out of our way, so we've stopped to see it.

An iron gate bars vehicles access to the village. A sign in the parking lot outside warns us not to leave anything visible in our cars. Another simple sign beside the pedestrian entrance gives a chronology of the awful fate that befell this town over half a century ago.

The trolley tracks still run down the cobblestone street, and I find myself half-consciously balancing on one as I walk, just as I did as a boy in my own town. The bulk of a roofless stone church looms up on the left. A rusted iron water pump rests in an alcove of a stone wall. A third sign, against the wall just beyond the alcove, commands in large letters, SILENCE.

There were rumors, heard at the pharmacy, that somewhere to the north, perhaps in Normandy, the Allies had in the last few days attempted a landing. There was no confirmation of it. Still, after four years of brutal German occupation, the idea was very exciting. If they could only get word from Oradour-sur-Vayres, they could be sure. That other Oradour, about 30 kilometers to the southwest, was a center of the Resistance, and would have radio contact.

The village lies gaping to the sun; not a roof is intact, except in two isolated outbuildings. Someone decided, some fifty years ago, to leave the town as nearly as possible as it was found on June 11, 1944. A wooden gate across each empty door opening gently dissuades souvenir hunters from entering. A small enamel plaque identifies the business or the home and its owner.

At two in the afternoon, the sound of approaching

motors suddenly filled the air. The villagers looked toward the gates to see the dreaded uniforms of a Nazi SS unit. The officer in charge pulled up in the square, while the troops fanned out through the village and ordered everyone out. The children were brought down from the schools; mothers arrived with infants in strollers; men came from their work; six luckless bicyclists passing through the village were also apprehended.

This used to be a hotel. Now it's four limestone walls, floored with shattered roof tiles and ashes slowly being overwhelmed by weeds and a small poplar tree. You can see where the second floor joists fitted into the masonry. The mason made his pockets properly, so that a collapsing joist wouldn't topple the wall. The hotel kitchen, against the rear wall, has a raised hearth fireplace with a swinging pot hanger. A blackened and cracked cast-iron cauldron sits in front of it on the floor. A charred sewing machine pokes up through ashes on a stone shelf. We gaze at all these artifacts of a vanished life through a threat of tears brimming constantly in our eyes.

By three o'clock everyone was assembled and surrounded in the square. The SS troopers herded all the women and children into the stone church, and the men into six barns located here and there around the village.

Even fifty years ago, the French used cast-concrete power poles. They stand now as they did then, and the trolley wires are still strung from each to the next all the way up the main street to the switches and the tiny car barn. Two rusting automobiles sit in the Renault garage where they burned, so long ago, and another rests on its wheel rims outside the pharmacy. A clanging noise turns my head. In a butcher shop, a set of balance scales hung on a hook bumps against the stone wall in the wind. A kid's bike, its tires and spokes melted away, lies crazily in an alley.

At four o'clock they started torturing and shooting the men in the barns. They barricaded the church doors and set it on fire with the women and 205 kids inside. Then they set the barns on fire and burned the entire village and 642 people. Only eight escaped—six men from one barn; one woman who climbed up onto the altar and dropped from one of the stained glass windows just above it; and the kid playing hooky.

If that kid's still alive, he's just about my age now. He'd be the only one still living from this town that was utterly destroyed in a case of mistaken identity. I wonder if he lives with regret or guilt that he is the only one. I wonder if he ever comes here to visit the two glass coffins filled with the ashes of his family and neighbors, the photographs of the town soccer team, the pocket watches fused forever at a quarter past four. Or the ultimate irony: the melted metal frame of an infant's stroller on the stone floor of the sanctuary.

The motto on the town gate reads, *"Souviens-toi!"* Remember what?—to hate the Nazis? Not to let this happen again? Why, it's happening still, somewhere else, at the very moment we're stumbling numbly through this open sore on the face of the earth. Why is our species, with its unique capacity to reach for the infinite, also the cruelest? How many towns like this will it take?

The answers were written long ago and, like the ashes of Oradour, are blowing in the wind.

I Need You Here! Now!

A SATURDAY MORNING IN MARCH: SNOW still on the ground, but even the nights beginning to stay warm. The time of year you put a few sticks of wood into the stove or the furnace first thing in the morning, just to cut the chill, then let the fire go out during the day. I was working that morning, down in town, helping my floor tile subcontractor lay out a big kitchen. The telephone rang. It wasn't my phone, but I could tell it was my ring; so I answered it.

"Will!" It was my wife. Her voice was tense with excitement. "There's smoke pouring out of the stove down in the shop, and the cellar's full of smoke! I need you here!"

"There couldn't be! I haven't had a fire in that stove for a couple of weeks."

"Doesn't matter. It's filling the house with smoke, and I need you here now!"

Over the years I've heard people of many different stripes claim there's a God who watches over us and protects us from harm. In the face of evidence both supporting and refuting that proposition, I'm willing to suppose it's possible. But wouldn't you think that if there were, he or she would at moments like this whisper into our inner ear, "I know as well as you do, my friend, that there's no fire. That's irrelevant. This is a test, like the ones the Federal Communications Commission does on the radio."

It was also like one of those College Board exams I took once. They give you a paragraph to read, and then suggest several interpretations. You're supposed to pick the right one. I did very well on College Boards. But that was long ago.

Any woman (she claimed later) could have seen instantly the real message in her summons: I need you here, my Comforter, my Protector and Shield Against Disaster! And I need you right now! But what I heard, otherwise engaged as I was, on the other side of town, seven miles away, was: "I need you here right now because there's a dangerous problem with the chimney, and I'm certain we're about to lose the house!" I knew there couldn't possibly be a dangerous problem with that chimney whose every block and brick I had counted, carried up a ladder, and helped lay, and whose flues were clean as whistles. So I logically concluded that she didn't need me there. She only wanted some assurance that everything was all right.

So I told her I'd take care of it and hung up. I found a phone book and tried to call a couple of responsible neighbors to go over and soothe her troubled mind. No luck; nobody home. So I called her back to see if things had settled down any.

"What!" she cried. "You're not on your way yet? I'm calling the fire department!" There was a click as she hung up, and it began to dawn on me that, real fire in the chimney or not, somebody's metaphoric fat was in the metaphoric fire—mine! I bid the floor tile guy adieu, hopped into my truck, and headed home quite a bit faster than usual.

A few hundred yards from the house, my rear-view mirror exploded with the blue lights of a police car. I pulled aside and rolled down the window to explain, but the cop just roared on by, pointing forward as he did. It occurred to me we might be headed to the same place.

Yep. There were a couple of pickup trucks in the road. There was the end of a four-inch hose wrapped around the black cherry at the foot of the driveway by the brook, and the big red tanker truck that had unrolled it was parked up at the top beside the house, surrounded by a bunch of guys in yellow coats. Mother, the dog, and the cat were in the yard, too, Mother in her bathrobe and my shoepacs, holding the portable phone. They all appeared to be having a great time. Behind me, as I climbed out of my truck and hurried up the hill, I could hear more sirens.

I was right, of course; there had been no danger. But I was dead wrong, also; that wasn't the point. She didn't want some neighbor telling her everything was all right. She wanted me there. That book about men from Mars and women from Venus, you know? That's it.

I'd put wood into the furnace, and it had ignited, just as it was supposed to. But it was so warm that morning, the damper had shut down, and the pile of wood had just smoldered. The wind and temperature had been just right, so some of the acrid smoke coming out the chimney had been sucked back down the adjoining flue, the one to the wood stove in the shop.

Then it had leaked in great gouts from the old-fashioned shop stove, floated up the cellar stair well, and touched off the alarm, which she had found unsettling. So she'd grabbed the animals, her purse, the portable phone, and my Sorels, and run out into the yard, where she'd been ever since.

But how and why, some of the firemen—all guys I knew; it was very embarrassing—how, they asked, could the smoke have gotten sucked back down a different chimney? Well, I suggested, it might have, if the guy who built it had neglected to install the cleanout door in the masonry opening at the foot of the flue and thus invited a downdraft. They nodded concurrence, and I could sense a tacit understanding among us that the next item of business for me that day—once I got Mother back into the house—was the purchase and installation of a little cast-iron cleanout door. Mother assured the assembled firemen and police that I would be making a healthy cash donation to the volunteer fire department that year. They rolled their eyes and poked me in the ribs one more time, rolled up their hoses, and left with a great roaring of diesel engines.

"There, you see?" I assured her when the echoes had finally died away. "No problem. Just a quirky wind current."

"That's not the point!" she cried. (I knew she would.) "The point is that, when I needed you, you weren't there for me!" I don't know where she gets that new-age granola talk. Probably from the television; everybody talks that way nowadays.

The next night, at a dinner party, I was talking with the guys about a summer canoe trip we're planning, and I could hear her telling her story to the women. When she finished, they all cackled for it must have been five minutes. Then she asked what would have happened in their houses in a similar situation: whether their husbands would have responded differently. And of course they all but one said, are you kidding? Sure, you bet, my old man would have come zooming right home! But there was something important missing from the question: None of those guys had built his own chimney and therefore could have been sure, as I was, that nothing dangerous could have gone wrong.

It didn't matter. They all stuck together. I knew they would. You can't teach or expect a woman to be logical.

The Three Bears

IN RECENT YEARS I'VE BEGUN TO NOTICE
that the other men in our hunting camp are treating
me with a deference I can impute only to my age; I'm
now the oldest man in camp. They ask if they may do
little things for me—hang my wet towel by the stove,
bring me a bottle of beer from the cold porch, or
carry my pack basket up to the sleeping loft. It's very
nice of them, and I do appreciate it. But it's a little
unnerving, too. Is it just respect, or do I appear
increasingly unable to do these things for myself?

During the daily hunts, they've lately begun
assigning me the easy routes and the nearby watches—the ones where traditionally you send adoles-
cents, incompetents, or senescents. That's all right,
except that most of the excitement usually occurs farther away from camp. My assignments are designed
primarily to help me feel I have something important
to do, and to plug one more hole through which a
desperate, fleeing deer conceivably might try to slip.
So I do it without a murmur, and usually freeze half
to death before the hunters finally come through,
hours later.

They did it to me again yesterday morning: stuck
me on a watch known as "the big yellow birch

halfway up the blazed line." It's an easy ten-minute trudge up there, and not a bad spot. You stand behind the tree and just peep out now and then to see if anything's moving out toward where the hunters are coming from. When I arrived at the watch, it was still too dark to see my sights. I trod down a little place in the snow for my feet, so there'd be no crunching or crackling of sticks if I did have to move quietly. Then I settled down to wait.

Just about first light, I heard something out in front of me, on the other side of the tree, rustling in the leaves. It wasn't a squirrel. Too early in the morning, and, besides, I could tell it was heavy. It was close!—maybe forty yards—and moving toward me. I just couldn't see it yet.

In a few minutes it got bright enough for me to see the cross hairs in my scope, so I kind of leaned to my left and peeked around that big yellow birch trunk in front of me. There was a huge chunk of black hair about the size of our old Volkswagen Beetle! It was a big sow bear. She had a good-sized cub with her. The two of them were scratching back the leaves and gobbling acorns, not even chewing them. They had absolutely no idea that I was there, but they were coming straight toward me, only about twenty feet away now, and one way or another they were going to find out very soon. I clicked off the safety of my rifle. They were making so much noise they didn't hear it.

I stuck my head and shoulders and the muzzle of my rifle out from behind the left side of the birch tree and said, nice and loud, "Morning, ma'am." She stopped short and looked up, with her nose twitching and her left front paw lifted up to her chest. The cub mimicked her perfectly. But they still didn't see me!

"Hi, there!" I waved my left hand a little, praying that, if she did come my way fast, it would be to my left. Bears are so quick, I'd never get turned around fast enough if she ran to my right.

Instead she just sat back on her haunches, raised up a little, and stood there sniffing and waving her muzzle back and forth. Then she lowered her head, got back down onto all four feet, and the two of them ambled past me and out across the flat toward Will Martin's notch. Every once in a while they stopped and looked back over their shoulders, the cub still aping exactly every move his mother made. I watched them there for three or four minutes. And then they were gone.

She had known!—known that I wouldn't try to harm either her or the kid! Somehow she had learned or sensed that I had no intentions hostile to her interests.

That hasn't always been so.

THE FIRST BOOK I can remember reading was *The Bears of Blue River*. It was written by Charles Major, I don't know when; but he died in 1913. I had an old, worn copy that had been my father's when he was a boy. By the time I finished with it, there was hardly a page still attached to the spine, and the borders of the illustrations were all smudged. The stories in it were about a kid named Balser Brent, maybe twelve or thirteen years old, who lived on the frontier, in Indiana, in the 1820s. Balser had an amazing propensity for crossing paths with very large and aggressive black bears, some of which seemed to have mystical properties. But, after hairbreadth escapes and sometimes grisly combat, he invariably managed to dispatch them all.

To this day I can recall the details of each of the battles—the Big Bear (Balser's first, which caught him unarmed out on the end of a floating log, fishing); the One-Eared Bear, hacked to death with a hatchet; and the dreaded, glow-in-the-dark Fire Bear, which disappeared, along with Balser's feeble-minded friend Polly, in a cataclysmic natural gas explosion.

It was pure romantic fantasy. But what's childhood for? I loved it, and dreamed of the day when I, like Balser, would myself possess "a smooth-bore carbine, ten pounds of fine powder, and lead enough to kill every living creature within a radius of five miles." It didn't occur to me that our neighbors in downtown Albany might find that a little antisocial. On the other hand, maybe not. The notorious gangster Jack "Legs" Diamond was shot to death in 1931 in his apartment only a block away from our own peaceful flat.

Whatever the neighbors might have thought about my ambitions, I think I sensed already at the age of six that I wouldn't be living in the city forever, and that someday, in some distant forest, I would myself encounter and slay many big black bears. That sense turned out to be prophetic. We moved out of the city two years later. I soon joined the Boy Scouts and began a love affair with the outdoors that has lasted all my life so far. And I encountered the bears, all right. But as for slaying them—that part of the scenario was pure fantasy.

I GOT MY FIRST chance when I was twenty. I worked that summer as what's called a "hut boy" in the Adirondacks, at a lodge about four miles up the trail to Mount Marcy. I kept the place clean, packed in food from town about five miles away, did a little cooking for hikers, and sold candy bars and trail maps. Like most lodges in those days, it had a garbage dump out in the woods; and like most garbage dumps, this one had a bear.

It came only at night and scattered trash all over the place, including the lawn. We needed a composting pit with a secure cover.

By chance, the club that owned the lodge had hauled in a new 275-gallon kerosene tank during the winter and installed it in a little tool shed in the yard just opposite the rear kitchen door and the back porch. The discarded tank was lying in the woods. So I cut the bottom out of it with a cold chisel, dug a pit, and sank it into the hole with its top flush with the ground. I made a couple of wooden covers for the openings in the top and had a nice, bearproof garbage facility.

At least that's what I thought. But a creature powerful enough to tip over a cast-iron cookstove, bite through soup cans, and tear screen doors off their hinges isn't much daunted by plywood garbage pit covers. So now, besides picking up my lawn every other morning, I had the chore of making new covers.

This was the chance I'd been waiting for. It wasn't quite the heroic confrontation I'd had in mind, and I didn't own my own rifle yet. But the forest ranger whose cabin stood half a mile down the trail lent me his lethal little .250-3000 carbine. I set it beside my bed, along with a headlight that strapped to my forehead, and waited impatiently to slay my first bear.

It came about midnight. I heard it crackling through the brush out behind the tool shed. Adjusting the headlight above my left eye and grabbing the gun, I slipped quietly out the kitchen screen door and squatted on the little back stoop, about two feet above the ground. I used to wear a red flannel nightshirt in those days and must have looked a little goofy out there. But it was dark as a closet, and there was no one else there, anyway. I bated my breath and waited.

Suddenly, there it was!—a surprisingly large dark shape, blacker even than the night, right between me and the tool shed, about five feet away! Its long, pointed nose was aimed right at my garbage pit, and I could hear its snuffling breath.

I must have moved slightly, or it must have scented me. Because all at once it stopped short, turned toward me, and reared right up on its hind legs. Its head was higher than mine; its blackness filled the whole space in front of me. Still squatting, I fell over backward against the screen door, the headlight irrelevant. I fired right at the black middle of the bear's body.

There was a bright stab of flame in the dark, then the tremendous roar of the gun in the quiet night. As the echoes died away, I heard the crashing of brush on the hill behind the shed and the pounding of my heart in my ears.

In the silence that followed, I heard a strange gurgling sound, like water from the pipe of a hillside spring. Then, in a horrible, slowly dawning awareness, I detected the distinctive aroma of kerosene! I had blown a nice quarter-inch hole right through the side of the shed and that brand-new oil tank.

IT WAS TWENTY YEARS more before I got another chance. During that time I'd finally got the rifle I'd dreamed of, my lovely little Winchester 94 carbine for which there's a provision in my will. I'd also started going to Old Charlie's deer camp in the Adirondacks to hunt with him and his boys.

Once in a while somebody up there would shoot a bear. I do remember having a vague feeling, whenever I saw one hanging on the buck pole, that there'd been no good reason for shooting it. We never ate any of it. Billy, one of Old Charlie's sons, did make a bear-claw necklace once, but its value as an item of jewelry was limited. It ended up as a hat band, I think. Then there was the problem of the way a bear looks when it's been skinned: so much like a man that you have to keep looking back to make sure there's a difference. In spite of all that, I was still hopeful. It was just a matter of time before I got one. Time was what I had lots of in those days.

In the fall of 1975, I took up hunting with a muzzle-loader before the regular deer season opened. It wasn't from any sportsmanlike impulse or a desire to emulate Daniel Boone—I can't see what's so sporting about blowing a half-inch diameter lead ball through an animal's hide and then, if you haven't killed it, making it wait for quietus while you fart around with powder, patch, ball, and ramrod. No, it wasn't for any of that. I just wanted to get out into the woods before the crowds.

I was down behind our old house on a hot, hazy October day. Loggers had hacked out all the white pine, left the red pine and soft maples standing, and the tops where they fell. Pretty messy, and the blackberries had come up thick. It was hard to get through there without making a lot of noise and getting all scratched up. In those conditions, you take only one careful step or two, then wait and look for a minute or two. Look for movement, shape, and color. Make sure your percussion cap is still on the nipple where it's supposed to be. I was doing just fine.

I had just moved to a spot at the base of a scraggly red pine about ten inches in diameter when, all at once, without any warning at all, dead branches and pieces of bark began to rain down on my head. I ducked, jumped back, and looked up. I thought the tree was coming down!

A small black bear was sliding down that tree like a fireman down a brass pole, and he was taking all the dead branches with him. He must have been watching me coming, and wondering if I saw him up there. When I had stopped right under him, he must have thought the jig was up, and he was making a break for it. The jig was up, all right. The percussion cap was right where it ought to be, and I was cool as a cucumber. I couldn't possibly miss.

He came down my side of the tree and hit the ground facing directly away from me: just the direction he wanted to go. But it didn't matter which way he went; he was mine. It wasn't going to be pretty. If that muzzle loader had been a thermometer, I could have taken that bear's temperature.

I cocked the hammer, aimed—just as twenty years before—right into the middle of the bear, and pulled the trigger. The percussion cap went off with a little "snap!" The powder charge, however, did not. I stood there gaping in the blackberry bushes, watching that black rump disappear and listening to that now familiar sound of crackling branches dying into the distance.

This was getting serious. I should have seen what was in the cards. But my dander was up; like Casey at the bat, I'd knock the next one out of the park.

It took another ten years. By that time, hunting had become for me more a ritual than a sport. I cherished the litany of the Friday evening drives across Vermont to hunting camp. I still hunted mostly alone in those days—up the blazed line, through Will Martin's Notch, then over onto Pincherry Mountain all day, and down past the old forge and Theriault's abandoned logging camp just about dark. One very cold Saturday morning just at daylight I slipped around the lower end of the oak ridge to the old log road up Beggs Brook (the summer folks, more poetic than we, call it Crystal Brook). I followed the road to the first side valley on the right.

It was cold! There was about four inches of fresh snow on the ground, and the sky had been clear all night. The temperature was still down below zero. That's not too bad if you're working hard, but when you're just sort of stealing along, it's hard to get the chill out from between your shoulder blades. Not to mention your hands are wrapped around seven pounds of frozen steel. So I worked as hard as I could climbing up the high bank at the side valley.

I got out my little piece of canvas and sat down on the steep part of the slope about ten feet below the break of the bank. From there I could see up and down Beggs Brook and up the side valley, too. I'd spot anything that moved for about eighty yards in three directions. A good spot.

But cold! I had on yellow cloth gloves that might as well have been ice packs. I guessed I could stand it till the sun came over the ridge of Giant. To divert myself, I silently recited "The Cremation of Sam McGee" and "The Hermit of Sharktooth Shoal." I started doing the old Charles Atlas dynamic tension exercises—legs, abdomen, chest and shoulders, and try to bend the rifle barrel with your hands. Then I did the isometric exercise recommended to me once by a football coach: tense up all your abdominal muscles, beginning with the diaphragm and working your way down to the sphincters (but be careful with the sphincters, he said, or you could be in trouble). If I didn't freeze to death first, at least I'd come back to camp looking like Johnny Weismuller.

It was very quiet. I could hear the brook bubbling under the ice way down below me, and feel my pulse at my temples. But all at once, after about twenty minutes, a red squirrel began to buzz and chirp right behind my left shoulder. You know the sound. It's a mixture of warning and outrage. How the devil could he have spotted me? I hadn't moved an inch for at least ten minutes.

Well, I stood it for another ten, and he wouldn't let up. Nothing was going to happen out in front of me as long as that went on behind me, and I was freezing, anyway. So I decided the hell with it, and stood up.

There was a tremendous explosion and crashing right behind me! I thought for a second that a dead tree had fallen over. Every hair on my head stood straight up. I spun around to my left, and there was a bear standing right there, about six feet away, all crumpled up into a strange kind of ball. But he was getting ready to run and didn't stay that way long.

You may have seen black bears start to run. In that split second between surprise and action, they plant their hind feet about six inches in front of their ears. Then when they uncurl, they're already doing about thirty miles an hour. I've always thought that if a human being could copy that start, he'd break the world record for the hundred meters, easy.

My gun came up as a reflex, but the bear wasn't there any more. He'd leaped right past me and was somersaulting head over heels down the steep hill toward the brook. But he had fifty yards to go to reach cover. I knew I had him. There were seven cartridges in that little carbine, and my mind was as cool as my body. At last! I thought. Ha ha! At last!

He reached the bed of the tributary brook and got to his feet to jump it. I fired. At the blast of the gun, he turned to his right about ninety degrees and started to hump up the far bank, angling upstream. A wide open shot. I fired again.

He disappeared into a thick clump of little hemlocks. I guessed where he'd come out, and got ready. I guessed right, and aiming more carefully this time, I fired again.

Again he turned ninety degrees to his right, tumbled into the brook, turned right again, and began angling up the near bank directly toward me. He had no more idea where he was going than he knew what was after him. He was just dying to get away from that awful noise and confusion. I laid the little gold bead of the front sight right on his head. Here we go! here we go!

He was about seventy-five feet away now, and I fired right into him. He was still coming! He hadn't looked like a very big bear as he'd run along the far bank of the brook, but now I was aware of the hump on his back, and with every jump toward me, that hump looked quite a bit bigger. I couldn't miss.

I levered in a new cartridge. And the gun jammed!

If you've used a lever-action rifle, you know what had happened. When you work the lever to eject the spent cartridge casing, the extractor pulls the shell backward out of the barrel until the front end of it clears the back end of the barrel. Then the ejector spring throws it out of the gun. A new cartridge snaps up into place, and you close the lever, sliding it into the firing chamber. Trouble is, the new cartridge is longer than the old, because it's still got a bullet sticking out the front of it. And if you've been in a big hurry and moved the lever only far enough back to throw out the old one, but not far enough to let in the new one, you're in a jam.

Some people say that moments like that, recalled later, seem to have happened in slow motion, like the violent scenes in a movie. I can't say that's what happened there. Things seemed to be happening awfully fast, and I can recall only a few details. I can recall the gun jamming, and my working the lever to free it. I can remember feeling increasingly frantic as my reactions began to fall behind the speed at which things were happening. I can see the flame of the explosion of my last shot coming out the barrel, which means that I must have been holding the rifle only waist-high. I can see the white metal of the carrier coming up from the magazine, instead of a cartridge—no more bullets! I can hear the labored blowing of that poor bear's breath coming closer. And I can feel my feet slipping out from under me, and myself falling on my ass into the snow.

The bear kept right on galloping, and galloped across my lower legs. As he went by, his eyes were rolled back in his head just like the eyes of a horse that's scared to death. His breath was rasping in his throat. Then there was his black rump. And then nothing. He disappeared over the bank to my left and crashed down toward Beggs Brook.

I was frantically digging in my left-hand pants pocket with my glove still on, trying to get hold of one last cartridge I knew was there. I heard someone shouting, "Hey, wait! Hey, wait!" and realized it was me. I pulled the cartridge out of my pocket, shoved it into the gun, and slammed the bolt shut—right on the end of the thumb of my glove.

He didn't wait. I got up and climbed very slowly back up to my piece of canvas, digging the cartridges from the snow as I went. I found five spent ones and two live ones.

Still pretty shaky, I reloaded with the three cartridges I now had left. I shook the snow off my canvas, folded it carefully, and put it into the game pocket on the back of my mackinaw. I reached into my warm inside shirt pocket, took out a Hershey bar, broke off four squares, stuck them into my mouth, and put the rest back. The cold was forgotten for the time being. I had a feeling that something important had just happened, as if I had been climbing a mountain and just emerged on an open ridge, from which I could see things previously unseen or undreamed of.

Following the tumbling track of the frantic bear, I slid down the bank to the old log road along the brook. The sun was just breaking over the high shoulder of Giant Mountain. I was going back to camp for coffee. Somebody was bound to ask me about all the banging over on Beggs Brook that morning. It was a difficult decision: Should I feign ignorance, or tell them I was shooting at a running deer too far off to hit? Or should I tell them the truth and spend the rest of my life being kidded about either poor shooting or bad lying? But I'm nothing if not a storyteller, and this was too good a story to hold inside. May the devil take the consequences.

I knew one thing for certain: Except perhaps in self-defense, I'd never shoot at another bear again as long as I lived. And in the uncanny way animals have of sensing our thoughts and intentions, I think the bears now know it, too.

Rona and Alice's Christmas

IT BEGAN SNOWING AROUND NOON. By the time Alice started home from work, there was already six inches on the ground. Big flakes streamed past her headlights. But her little Escort, its front wheels spinning and throwing up snow on both sides, made it up the hill all right. She didn't dare stop at the mailbox for fear she might not get started again. Easing off the gas as the front wheels struck the dry gravel inside the shed, she coasted to a stop.

"Might 's well go get the mail long as I got my boots on," she thought. Setting her small bag of groceries on the kitchen steps, she trudged out to the road. In the mailbox were a magazine and a few envelopes. She carried them in with the groceries, kicked off her boots, switched on the kitchen light, and turned up the thermostat.

This was always the worst moment of the day: coming home to the cold silence of the empty house. Ray's old blue denim frock still hung on its hook by the back door, and his .22 stood in the corner behind the door. But he would never again be coming home for supper.

It had been so close! After forty-two years, they had just two more to go, and they both could have retired. Exactly six months ago, she reflected—June

21st, the longest day of the year—Ray's boss had called her at the office just before two in the afternoon. "Alice," he said, "I think Ray's had a heart attack. They just took him over to the hospital. I think you better get over there."

The longest day of the year. Now here it was the shortest day, long dark outside at six o'clock, and she was sitting in the kitchen at suppertime without an appetite. The garbage bag needed to go out; the pile of newspapers in the corner was higher than she could remember it ever being before. The snow hissed against the window.

"Dammit, Ray!" she said out loud. "You got off easy compared to this!" She started picking through the mail. The magazine was addressed to Ray—R. A. Lamott. *Popular Mechanics.* She set it aside. There were a couple of Christmas cards; she put them on a pile of unopened cards by the window. Then a couple of bills and a letter from Norman Foster addressed to Ray. Norman was a retired schoolteacher who owned a little farm about a mile down the road, but rented it out and spent most of the year in Florida.

"Dear Ray," it began. "Thanks again for taking care of the plowing at my place last winter. Trust you can do it again this year. I've enclosed a check that should cover it. If it doesn't, let me know, and I'll send more.

"Awful glad you can do this for me. The young couple who rent the place have several kids, but no phone, so they need to be able to get out in case of emergencies. Hope you and Alice have a wonderful Christmas. All the best, Norman."

"Oh, no!" said Alice. "The plowing!" For years Ray had plowed several driveways in the neighborhood with his big pickup, which still stood beside her Ford in the shed. Alice had called Larry Hart from the service station to come hook up the plow just before Thanksgiving so she could keep her own driveway clear. It had never occurred to her that somebody else might be counting on it. But of course Norman didn't know Ray was dead, so he—and his tenants—were still expecting him.

"Well, why don't I go down?" she said. "I'm not hungry, anyway, and it's got to be done. Maybe I'll feel better if I do something physical." She put on her coat, boots, hat, mittens, and scarf, scuffed out to the far end of the shed, and pulled herself up onto the high seat of the truck. It started hard, but finally caught with a familiar roar. She raised the plow, backed out, and headed slowly down the road.

There was no car in the driveway of the little farm, but there were lights inside. She could see a decorated Christmas tree through the misted windows. She'd just plow them out and go on home, she decided, without stopping inside. They'd think it was Ray. Then tomorrow she'd call Norman and have him make other arrangements.

Just as she made her first pass up to the garage, the big pickup suddenly coughed and died. She tried the starter. It ground fruitlessly. She peered at the gas gauge. Empty. For the second time that night she said, "Dammit, Ray!" and then laughed out loud at how much it sounded like her old self. She could just hear him saying, "God, I'm sorry, Alice! I was gonna get some on my way home." But he had died first. So she slid out of the cab and stumped up to the side door of the little house.

A young woman answered her knock. She was dressed in jeans and a blue chambray shirt with the tail out. She wore glasses, and her hair was in a kerchief. "Oh!" she said, startled, "I thought it was Mr. Lamott."

"I'm Alice Lamott," said Alice, "and I'm afraid I'm out of gas. You don't happen to have a gas can around anywhere, do you?" Behind the young woman, she could see three little boys peeking at her from the living room. They wore jeans, too, and undershirts stained with food. On their upper lips were brown mustaches of cocoa.

"Gas?" said the woman. "Gosh, I don't know. Let me look in the cellar. I know Frank used to keep some cans down there. Oh!"—she stuck out her hand—"I'm Rona Hickey." She switched on the cellar light and disappeared down the stairs. Alice, her boots covered with melting snow, stayed where she was, on the mat just inside the door.

The boys edged into the room. Alice guessed them to be about nine, six, and four. They stood shyly, leaning against the living room door jamb and the refrigerator, looking at her.

Suddenly the little one asked her, "Are you Mr. Lamott's girlfriend?"

Alice was startled. "Well . . . uh, I guess so, sort of," she answered.

"My daddy has a girlfriend, too," continued the four-year-old in a rush. "That's why he isn't here."

The nine-year-old turned on him angrily. "Jimmy, you shut up!"

"Well, he does . . ." Alice, stunned into silence, was glad to hear Rona Hickey's footsteps coming

57

back up the stairs. She was carrying a two-gallon can.

"I think this is gas. I don't know if it's regular or what, but it ought to work."

"Thanks," said Alice, turning to go out. "I'll get it filled and bring it back."

"Oh, no rush. We don't need it for a while. You have time for a cup of coffee when you get done? I'll make some."

"Uh . . . sure. I'll come back in soon as I'm finished."

A few minutes later, sitting in the steaming, littered kitchen, Alice poured milk into her coffee and stirred it while Rona chattered. It had been a long while, obviously, since she'd had anybody to talk to. The words just streamed out of her.

Frank had moved out in the middle of October and was living over in Benton. He was still working, so he brought her money every week and they were able to live. But she had no car or telephone, and they'd have to move as soon as she could find another place. It looked as though they were not going to be together for Christmas for the first time in twelve years.

"Us, too," said Alice. "Ray died back in June. This'll be my first Christmas alone, too."

"Oh!"—Rona's eyes were huge behind her glasses—"I didn't know that!"

"Yep. Twenty-first of June. So I guess we're kind of in the same boat, you might say." She spoke with an affected toughness that she did not feel; but then, for the first time seeing the whole picture before her—the piles of dirty dishes and laundry, the three soiled little boys, and the moist-eyed young woman—she suddenly felt the shell around her dissolving. "Oh, God!" she exclaimed. "Isn't it awful when they go!"

Rona bit her lower lip and nodded. But when she nodded, tears suddenly began spilling out of her in a flood. She put her head down on her arms and sobbed, her shoulders shaking.

Without knowing how she got there, Alice found herself sitting beside Rona with her arm around her shoulders. Little Jimmy's arm, coming from somewhere on the other side of Rona, lay on top of hers. "I'm sorry, Rona," said Alice. "I'm sorry. It'll work out all right."

In a few minutes Rona stopped shaking, lay quiet, and finally raised her head. Her glasses were full of tears and so misted that her eyes were invisible. Embarrassed at how she must look, she pulled the glasses off and wiped at her eyes with her shirttail.

"Look, I've got an idea!" said Alice. "I've got to go get some gas for the truck, anyway, in case I have to plow again. Why don't you all get cleaned up and dressed, and we'll go get a hamburger and French fries and a shake? We can all fit in the front seat of the truck."

That was the start of it. Two nights later Alice and Rona went shopping together for presents. On Christmas morning Alice got up early and drove down to the Hickeys'. Jimmy met her at the door, wide-eyed. "You . . . you should see . . ." he began. "You should see what Santa Claus brought!"

Later in the day, Rona and the three boys walked up to Alice's for dinner. Alice had decorated the kitchen and the table with balsam boughs and red velvet bows and roasted a turkey. Halfway through dinner, as Jimmy spilled gravy on the tablecloth for the second time, she looked up at the wedding picture of her and Ray on the sideboard. "Dammit, Ray!" she muttered softly. "I wish you could just see this!"

Harold Watermelon

THE VINALHAVEN FERRY MADE AN extraordinary stop, nosing into the pier at Hurricane Island with a cargo of new Outward Bound students. They stepped off onto the dock with an affected casualness, lugging their duffel bags. The Course Director stood atop a discarded wooden wire spool, clipboard in hand, and read off their names and watch assignments. Each of us instructors—watch officers, we were called—stood by the sign for his watch and greeted his students as they came up. At length I had all of mine, standing before me in an expectant semicircle. Unbelieving and aghast, I studied their faces, luggage, and costumes. It appeared at first glance that Admissions had screwed up royally. By the time we'd spent a day together, I was sure of it.

One of the most religiously observed features of the Outward Bound program, in its standard public courses, is its mixing of students of differing races, backgrounds, economic situations, and abilities. As these conscious mixtures of people work their way through the course, tackling and overcoming progressively difficult challenges, the individuals within them develop (at least in theory; a lot depends upon the instructor) a rapport with each other and, by extension, an appreciation of cultures and individuals unlike themselves.

I showed them their tents and told them to meet me as a group in half an hour at the main pier. They arrived precisely on time, ready for whatever challenges I might have in store. With great apprehension I sat on a large chunk of granite beside the pier and peered into the bright, eager faces clustered around me, hanging on my every word. There were twelve of them, a standard-size watch. But every one of them was so clearly upper- and upper-middle-class, so obviously intelligent and articulate, so thoroughly Anglo-Saxon! I had nobody from Dorchester, Southie, or the Bronx. Nobody scratching in the dirt with a stick, pretending to be ignoring me. Nobody looking over the edge of the high pier at the water far below and asking if we really were going to jump off the next morning at six o'clock.

They wore T-shirts and sweat suits emblazoned with *Groton* and *Taft* and *Exeter*, and one even sported a Marblehead Yacht Club cap. Desperately I scanned their chests, looking for at least one municipal high school. No soap. I did at last spot one kid from Minnesota, but even his sweat shirt read, *North Shore Country Day*. There was no hope for this course. Even the patron saint of our watch, for whom it was named—Fridtjof Nansen, the Norwegian polar explorer and Nobel Peace Prize winner—had had blond hair and blue eyes! So, for that matter, did I.

I was supposed to teach this gang to sail a thirty-foot open pulling boat? Already I'd heard them chatting among themselves about the Bermuda Race. I'd asked them all to bring notebooks and pencils, bathing suits, and towels to this meeting, and to my chagrin, nobody had forgotten or rebelled. How were we ever going to learn anything this way? The course stretched out before me, in my imagination, as a dreary succession of dry, seamless, polite successes. I racked my brains for some way to introduce a little dissonance, a little challenge, a little unexpected stress to this gang of eager beavers. In my distress, I must have prayed a little; for suddenly it came to me, like lightning from a clear blue sky.

"Gentlemen," I began (two of them were actually ready to take notes!), "the people in the admissions office have notified us watch officers of a very unusual situation, and they've asked us to discuss it with our watches. They have a student who has some special physical needs. He would like very much to take the course, but admissions is unwilling to assign him to a watch unless that watch is willing to accept him."

"What's wrong with him?" asked the Loomis sweatshirt.

"He's quadriplegic. He can't speak, and he literally cannot move a muscle to help himself do anything. But he wants to do this course, as much of it as he can, in any way he can. His family is against it. They're afraid he might be injured. But they've been persuaded to let him try, if a watch will agree to accept him."

I could see that my little speech had taken much of the bloom off the rose of their sailing and rock-climbing vacation. But I also knew I had them; noblesse oblige ran as strongly in their veins as dependent clauses in their conversation.

"Sir," said St. Paul's, "I'm sure I speak for the others. Nansen Watch will take him." The others assented, if a bit uneasily.

"Your spirits shine through you," I congratulated them. ("Excuse me, sir," piped up Exeter, "but isn't that from *Macbeth*?" It was.) They went through their morning activities discussing how they would handle the needs of their new watchmate. That afternoon I sent the food service gofer to the mainland for the biggest watermelon he could find. He brought back a 45-pounder. And that evening after supper I introduced it to the group. I gave it an Anglo-Saxon name, of course. No sense shaking anybody up too much.

"Gentlemen, this is Harold. By your invitation, he is now a full-fledged member of Nansen Watch. His needs are few, and his abilities are nil—except that he can float in water. He has expressed a fervent desire to participate in all the activities of the course—morning run and dip, rock climbing, initiative tests, ropes course, seamanship and navigation, the three-day solo, and final expedition. I will add to that only my fervent hope that, twenty-six days from now, he will still be with us, will have gone through everything with us, and will have no more scratches or bruises upon him than there are on any of you."

You can't imagine the relief on their faces. (They'd been working on a plan for sharing sanitary duties.) But future leaders of the people that they were, within moments they were scanning the course syllabus, planning how to get Harold unscathed through each of the activities ahead. They devised a sling from foam sleeping pads, towels, and a piece of canvas. In this sling, hanging from one pair of straining shoulders or another, Harold jounced around the rugged shoreline each morning at 5:30. Shedding the sling at the main pier, he then leaped twelve feet into the ocean in the arms of one of his watchmates. The first morning, we discovered that falling watermelons sink much farther underwater than falling people; we thought for a minute we'd lost them both.

Harold did everything. He climbed vertical granite cliffs in his sling, and he went cruising far down east. Somehow Nansen Watch managed to get him over "The Wall," and through the ropes course, strung through the trees far off the ground. His closest companion happened to be the boy who would have been lowest on the totem pole of physical ability but for Harold's presence. Harold appeared to have a wonderful time, and got a certificate and a pin at the end of the course.

But most of all, he taught his new friends the value of a metaphor, which is virtually all he was. They had thought the challenges of Outward Bound were real, but they turned out to be simply metaphors for real life. Their final evening on the island, as the fourteen of us sat in our circle for the last time, we talked about whether life itself might be one, too.

Next morning they waved from the rail as the ferryboat pulled away. Harold and I were left sadly behind on the pier. I waved after them for both of us. If we could have, Harold and I would have shaken hands with each other. Instead, I just gave him a big hug. Then I took him in his sling down to the north end of the island, cut him into quarters, and left him as an offering to the wild birds of the sea.

Canada Geese

Canada goose (Branta canadensis) Size 22–43 inches. Quite variable, with several different races. Grayish-brown above; cheek patches white; base of black "stocking" neck clearly defined against whitish underbody; bill and legs black. Lives in ponds, rivers, bays, and fields. Usually flies in V formation. In flight, black neck stretched out and usually curved downward. Very vocal. Normally mates for life. Breeds from Arctic coast south to Gulf of St. Lawrence; winters from Great Lakes and Nova Scotia south to Gulf of Mexico.

During the night the rain finally let up, and the October morning broke cool, gray, and damp. Perfect weather for shingling my roof—and with winter waiting in the wings, no time to waste. All morning I lugged bundles of asphalt shingles up the ladder and nailed them down. As I did, the wind slowly swung around to the west, then the northwest, strengthening by the hour.

Before three o'clock my fingers were freezing, and I was beginning to wonder if I could last till my planned quitting time of 4:30. "Hang in there, old feller!" I cheered. "What's an hour and a half?" Braced by that cheerful question, I pounded away—cutting, fitting, spreading stiff black cement—and dreamed of mugs of sweet, hot coffee and bathtubs full of steaming water. The radio hanging at the top of the ladder did its two cents' worth to help, playing—of all things!—a Bing Crosby retrospective, including "Blue Hawaii."

A few minutes after three, I noticed that I was listening for something else. It must have been the combination of the cold and the freshening north wind that did it. I found myself pricking up my ears and tuning into something beyond the steel guitars and Bing's baritone . . . something that I instinctively expected to hear; even though I wasn't quite sure yet what it was.

Then, at just the moment I remembered, I heard it: a very faint, half-imagined gabbling and barking, borne on the gale from Canada and seeming to come out of an empty sky. I slipped my hammer into the loop on the right side of my apron, stood up on the staging plank, and waited, searching the clouds at the edge of the bare treetops. The honking grew louder and more distinct, and suddenly there they were—a long, wavering wedge of Canada geese, only a couple of hundred feet above the trees, their rumps to the icy north wind and their bills pointed toward Long Island Sound. With the boost from the cold front, their speed must have been close to one hundred miles an hour, and they'd probably make it by nightfall.

In a few moments the last goose in the long line disappeared behind the trees and the honking died away, leaving me standing there rooted to my spot like a Neanderthal, holding a handful of galvanized shingle nails, knees black with roof cement, and torn by an almost irresistible desire to throw it all down and race to join them.

I don't know what the sight of migrating geese does to you, but it always leaves me misty-eyed and thoughtful, feeling poignantly the pull of gravity upon my booted feet, and dreaming of lost and botched opportunities. Their calling from the sky, as they fly to and from the Arctic each spring and fall, must strike some resonant chord in our dimmest memories. For the geese were here long before we were, their ancestral flyways engraved into their genes hundreds of years before the first wandering descendants of Ice Age man stumbled across the east coast of North America. And they'll be here long after we're gone. Other eyes than ours will search the sky when the first faint honking comes blowing down the wind.

THE FALL OF 1963, as I remember, was milder than usual, and the geese were late coming south. Friday, November 22, was another gray, damp day in our little town on the eastern edge of the Adirondacks. I was still teaching school then, and about two in the afternoon was presiding over a restless, squirming roomful of kids in a high school study hall. They were all thinking about the big soccer game that afternoon and the dance that evening. My own thoughts were on the weekend I'd be spending in hunting camp. And then, suddenly, the public address system broke in with the awful, incredible news from Dallas.

There would be no soccer game, and no dance. I

did go to hunting camp, most of all to get away from the unbearable, ghoulish immediacy of the television coverage of a nation in shock. But I could not bring myself to think of firing, much less even carrying, my rifle that weekend. When I picked it out of the rack in my study, it felt like a poisonous snake in my hands.

Late that Friday night the wind shifted. On Saturday, while my wife and her troop of Girl Scouts watched at home the preparations for the state funeral and then the murder of Lee Harvey Oswald, I sat on a windy, north-facing mountainside—shivering, overcome by successive waves of grief and rage—and watched the geese fly past. Flock after flock, tens of thousands of geese, streamed south out of the St. Lawrence Valley, set their course past the mountains by the distant loom of Lake Champlain, and headed for the upper end of the Hudson River flyway. A couple of days later, while a still-stunned, weeping nation buried its murdered President at Arlington, the geese would be paddling and feeding just a few miles away, in the shallows of the Chesapeake Bay. And thousands of years later, long after the eternal flame over the President's grave has been extinguished and forgotten, their children's children to hundreds of generations will be doing the same, little heedful of passing human events.

Wouldn't it be wonderful if we, as a species, could stop for just a few minutes whatever it is we're doing, and look up at the sky? If we could catch the beat of that rhythm, older than history, and understand that this is the way things were meant to be? If we could bequeath our children not an urge to get ahead, to achieve security, to get theirs?—but instead just to be, and to let their imaginations soar to the call of wild geese flying?

Hepburn Island

THIS IS THE WAY THE WORLD LOOKED before there was anybody to look at it.

In the beginning, there was the wind. There still is, almost all the time. Today it blows strong and cold from the northwest under gray, overcast skies. It carries the smell of far-off ice and the sound of heavy surf on solid rock. We're standing at the narrow end of a funnel formed by Dolphin and Union Strait, Amundsen Gulf, the Beaufort Sea, and beyond that, the Arctic Ocean. Here on the western saddle of the island, the short clumps of dry sedge wave stiffly as the concentrated wind blows through them. My Gore-Tex parka hood rattles behind my head like the sound of raindrops beating against a tent.

Soon after the beginning, there was also the rock. We tramp over dark, grayish-red basaltic granite more than five hundred million years old, formed during the first faint glimmerings of the dawn of life in the seas, when lava burst through a crack in the earth's crust and flowed across the land, hundreds of feet deep, for hundreds of miles. Hadrynian Diabase, the geological maps call it, in their incomparably dry manner of classification. Diabase is a good word for it. It expresses its great weight and suggests that it's the basement floor of the earth. Yet just beneath it, when we poke around at the base of its great, colum-nar cliffs, we find sedimentary rocks still more ancient, in which lie whispered mysteries: the tubu-lar tunnels of worms; basketball-sized calcareous spheres of the oldest algae ever found, laid open by erosion like onions sliced into halves; and faint, scratchy tracks in lithified mud, inexpressibly old, where trilobites once fluttered across the ocean floor.

Behind us, the basalt rises in a roughly polished dome about 350 feet high, grooved and sanded smooth by glaciers only 50,000 years ago. In the win-tertime, covered with snow, it looks from a distance like a giant igloo; thus its native name—*Igluhugyuk.* Rain water pools in pockets on its solid stone surface. Where the water has seeped down here and there into the columnar fracture planes of the rock, freez-ing has pushed up long, slender fragments in round clumps two and three feet high, like the petals of paper roses. I call them stone flowers.

Then there are the animals, who arrived perhaps two thousand years ago. There aren't many; the island is only nine miles long and less than a mile and a half wide for most of its length. The distance to the mainland is seven miles, and the water temperature thirty-eight degrees Fahrenheit. Probably not many mammals—and certainly no small ones—swim back and forth. But for eight months of the year the sea is ice-covered and solid.

Looking around, it's hard to imagine why any ani-mal would choose this bleak, exposed rock over the relatively lush valleys of the mainland. But some have. Trudging over the lumpy tundra, we come across caribou antlers every minute or so—some of them shed naturally and lying singly, but a surprising number paired and still attached to skulls. One set is quite fresh, with skull, cervical vertebrae, and scapulae still articulate. Foxes—not wolves; the big bones are uncracked—have scattered the rest in a circle about thirty feet in diameter. Like Matthew Brady after a Civil War battle, we pull enough of them together for a photograph.

Here and there lie the miniature cow pies of musk oxen, so they're here, too. We've been told there's been a bear out here, as well; native visitors have spotted its tracks. In nine square miles of land without a single tree and hardly a shrub, it's hard to believe we haven't spotted either. But the island is chopped up with cliffs and gullies everywhere, plenty of places to hide, from both human beings and the north wind. So on this gray, cold day nothing moves on the land but the grass, and out on the water, nothing but breaking waves flashing white against a metal-gray sea.

The European name Hepburn Island was given to it on July 24, 1821, by Leftenant (later Sir) John Franklin of the Royal Navy during his voyage along the coast with two large birch-bark canoes and a crew of nineteen—three officers, thirteen French-Canadians, two Inuit interpreters, and Ordinary Seaman John Hepburn. But Hepburn was no ordinary seaman. He bore the brunt of the heavy domestic chores of the expedition and time and again saved its officers from calamity. Three months after passing this place, one of the officers and ten of the men were dead of starvation, exhaustion, murder, and execution. Hepburn survived to return to England

and, thirty years later, join an expedition looking for the remains of Franklin's last, fatal expedition. He deserved to have a bigger island than this named after him. But this starkly beautiful bulwark against the heavy seas from the north—my favorite place on earth—is appropriate to his memory.

The wind, the rocks, and the animals are as they've been since before time began. Then, a little more than a thousand years ago, people arrived. For them as for the animals there was no sense of linear time, only a cyclical change of seasons and sources of food. *The People*, they called themselves, and were aware of no others. A thousand years ago, during a five hundred-year-long climatic optimum, the polar ice retreated and the Northwest Passage was briefly open during the summers. Whales were able to pass back and forth from the Bering Sea to Baffin Bay. The People ate their meat, blubber, and skin, and used their great bones, in a treeless land, to frame their subterranean houses. They lived in utter isolation from the rest of the world—were born, lived their whole lives hunting and fishing, and died and were buried here, somewhere among the rocks.

We call them the Thule. They've been extinct now for over six hundred years, victims of the Little Ice Age that gripped the northern hemisphere around 1400, closed the passage to whales, and extinguished the Viking settlements in Greenland. The animals that could migrate moved southward, inland. The Thule simply disappeared. Their circular, stone-walled houses slowly rotted back into the earth, and the island was left to the wind and the rocks.

Years ago, browsing through a 1968 edition of the

Pilot of Northern Canada, published by the Canadian Hydrographic Service, I came cross this almost passing reference in the description of Hepburn Island's magnificent harbor: "At the head of the harbour a narrow, shallow channel leads into a lake-like inlet which extends to the north side of the island and only a narrow, but fairly high, ridge prevents the island from being cut in two. Signs of early inhabitants exist here in the form of houses, partly constructed of bone, now caved in and covered with soil."

A few years later, at the end of a canoe trip down to the Arctic coast, I had a chance to look for those caved-in houses. In the few hours available, I climbed up and over the cliffs and round-topped dome of the island. Where would I camp, I asked myself, if I were staying here long and depending on the sea for food? It would be near fresh water and fuel; and there would have been both native willow and driftwood during that warm climatic phase. It would be out of the worst of the wind, yet near enough to rocky, high ground to get away from the worst of the mosquitoes in the summer. Near a sheltered cove for the skin boats, but with a view of the sea for spotting whales.

Remembering that the sea was much higher here one thousand years ago, I spotted half a dozen likely places and tramped to them. Nothing; only glacial boulders and ice-split rocks lying in a random jumble. I walked the narrow neck of the island, thinking, if I were a hunter, I would live here, where the large animals, moving, would have to pass close by. Still nothing. Half a mile away, in the protected cove on the south shore, every cast of a bright spoon catches a two-pound tomcod. Very poor eating. They look and taste like soggy toilet paper. But there was a group of Inuit, over on Victoria Island not so long ago, who were known as the Tomcod Eaters. So I prowled down around the cove. There I found only the remains of contemporary native hunting trips—splintered caribou femurs, rusted tin cans, and empty cartridges. Up on a ledge, inaccessible except by a perilous reach from above, lay a cache of rusty fox traps. I climbed up to take a look. Right beside them was an abandoned robin's nest with two dead fledglings in it—the postscript to a sad story that no one will ever hear. Besides that, still nothing. Only the wind and the smell of wet ice far out to sea. A fine mist condensed above the cold sea water, filtered through the sedge, and clouded my spectacles. I quit the search until another day that I was pretty certain would never come.

But it has. Almost by chance, I'm here again. And today, forsaking the logic that failed me last time, my friend Baird and I decide to follow the shoreline as far as we can in the time we have, and see what we can. Without knowing how, I know that today we're going to find the Thule. I know that generations of them are buried here among the rocks. I can feel their whispering spirits all around us.

We start at the isthmus, the narrow, two-sided beach that bars the surf of the Arctic Ocean from the quiet harbor on the other side, and walk eastward along the north shore. The surf breaks well offshore and booms on the black-boulder beach. Spray drives across our faces. For half a mile we pass only the sad detritus of invisible civilization: driftwood boards from boats and buildings, bits of Styrofoam picnic coolers, and a yellow plastic four-liter oil container. Then we mount a little headland. Ahead of us stretches a forbidding foreshore: solid, north-facing black ledge dipping into the surge; behind it, a few hundred yards of rough meadow; and behind that, more cliffs and ledges rising to the three-hundred-foot-high spine of the island. A golden eagle skims the crest of the spine, turns into the wind, and settles heavily onto a boulder, with a careful folding of wings, to watch us. More charmed by the stark beauty of the place than hopeful of finding any evidence of the Thule, we walk slowly along the ledge, the beginning and the end of the earth.

"What's that?" asks Baird suddenly, pointing toward the meadow.

"Couple of logs sticking up, looks like."

"But there aren't any logs here." He's right. We walk faster than usual. And there they are! Slabs of flat rock, almost like slate, that someone long ago stuck into the ground in a circle, or rather more in the shape of a light bulb. The area inside the bulb was excavated about two feet deep and flagged with more rock slabs. A chunk of driftwood, thicker than my leg and rotted away beyond divining its use, lies in the grass growing between the slabs. A large piece of bone, bigger than any in a caribou or even a bear, spans the entryway of the light bulb. We've found them.

But what an awful place to live! Even allowing for the warmer climate a thousand years ago, to live on an exposed north shore! They must have had some reason to want to be here. A small, rocky island just offshore breaks the surf a bit. It wouldn't be impossible to launch a boat in its lee. And the rocks of the small island are streaked with guano, suggesting another attraction in season. Where did they get their fresh water? I straighten up and look around. There's a depression about thirty yards behind us, a watercourse running down from a pond several hundred yards above. I walk over to see if it's big enough to drink from. As I approach the edge of the bank above the brook, the water comes to life upstream and down. Big spawning arctic char, as long as my arm, splash frantically away from my silhouette.

I wish we had more time. I'd like to camp here for several days and see what they saw, perhaps even feel what they felt when there was no one else in the world but this handful of people clinging to life on the northern edge of everything. But my impatient watch tells me it's time to go. We have to be over a hundred miles away by tomorrow afternoon to catch a plane, and the boat is waiting. Baird and I start back over the rocks toward the harbor.

But one last time I pause on the cliffs and look south. Seven miles away through the mist looms the shore of North America, my home continent. For some reason, I find the sight strangely moving. Through a mist of my own I promise that somehow I'll be back here again, and pitch my tent in a campsite chosen by another wanderer a thousand years ago. The wind will be here waiting.

A Damyankee in Texas

EVERY TIME I LEAVE MY RENTAL CAR parked almost anywhere in Texas, I return to find somebody's stuck a tract or a broadside or an appeal for money under one of my windshield wipers. This time it was after a protracted lunch with our children and two grandchildren in a Mexican restaurant in Tyler. Every car in the parking lot had a sheet of paper stuck under the driver's wiper, facing in.

There are many problems in the HEATHEN COUNTRY *called America, once known as a Christian nation. To name a few: rampant divorce; epidemic fornication; reckless useage of drugs and alcohol; social diseases; . . . open homosexual relationships; restrictions on prayer and attacks on Christian values; pornographic magazines . . . We have become a society of permissiveness and dullness, void of understanding. We have become so dull and so permissive, that many are willing to elect as a leader of this country, the person or persons pictured above.*

Pictured above was a grinning Bill Clinton trying on a beautiful white Stetson hat while an applauding Ann Richards (former governor of Texas) and some other politician I didn't recognize joined in the laughter. They seemed to be enjoying themselves thoroughly.

The above picture depicts his attitude . . . one that lacks sobriety; seriousness, concern . . . I don't see any of these words of wisdom possessed by any of the above.

(I very much dislike the smug and sarcastic practice of using [sic] to point out an obvious mistake. So I won't do it here; but I'll be as careful as I can to type any quotations exactly.)

Driving through Texas, from Abilene to Tyler; sitting in restaurants and diners, listening; reading the local papers, wondering; I've been absorbing the atmosphere of this great state. And I'm feeling very much like a stranger in the kingdom. Every time I'm tempted to put in my two cents or write a letter to the editor, I just advise myself, "You just keep your head down and your lip zipped, you pointy-headed, liberal, damyankee boy, and you may survive this trip intact." And I've been taking the advice, too. So far, so good.

YOU WOULD THINK THAT THERE ARE A FEW PEOPLE THAT WOULD TRY TO STOP THIS NATION FROM TURNING TO SOCIALISM. IT IS PRETTY PLAIN THAT IT DON'T WORK. ASK THE PEOPLE THAT HAVE LIVED UNDER IT. WE USED TO HAVE A GOVERNMENT THAT WAS THE ENVY OF THE REST OF THE WORLD. WE HAD AS MUCH FREEDOM AS ANY PEOPLE EVER HAD. THEN OUR EGG HEADS DECIDED THAT IT WAS NOT GOOD FOR THE PEOPLE TO BE FREE. THEY SAID THAT WOULD NEVER WORK. THE ONLY WAY THAT WE

WOULD EVER BE FREE WAS TO LIVE USER THEIR CON-
CEPT OF GOVERNMENT . . . WELL, YOU ARE GETTING
A TASTE OF IT. HOW DO YOU LIKE IT? . . . THERE IS
ONE ENDANGERED ANIMAL IN THIS NATION. THE
POOR SAP THAT WILL WORK FOR A LIVING OR AT
LEAST TRY TO MAKE A LIVING WORKING.

> *From "Just Thinking," a column by Sam Ringler
> in the Texas County News.*

Well, that got me to wondering: Why have places
like Texas developed such powerful negative feelings
about their federal government and the lives and
morals of people in other parts of the country? You'd
think that, living way up in New England, we swamp
Yankees would feel alienated from the self-impor-
tant bustle and purported corruption of, say, Wash-
ington, D.C. And I'm sure a lot of us do. But I've
never experienced anywhere else in the United States
anything like the anti-government, anti-"liberal,"
anti-intellectual virulence that seems common here
among the common folks. It's as if every problem or
shortcoming is someone else's fault—someone else
who is deliberately and surreptitiously trying to
undermine our American, Christian way of life.
You'd think that Christians, considering what
they've got to look forward to, would be among the
world's happiest people. But it sure doesn't sound
that way.

It's too damn bad, too. This is beautiful country,
once you get away from the sprawl and out into the
hills and hinterlands. I spent some months working
here, long ago, and remember with nostalgia the hot,
breathless mornings of midsummer; the starry nights

over open country with no other visible lights, Cano-
pus hanging red on the southern horizon; buzzards
floating overhead, jackrabbits racing the truck down
the lane; and during the fury of a December storm,
the radiance of the little box stove in the kitchen. I
recall feeling a little jolt, back then, when the local
Presbyterian minister referred to me jokingly as a
damyankee. But I don't remember hearing then any
of the unremitting anger I hear now. I can't help but
wonder—because anger doesn't seem to me like a
natural state of affairs—how much the federal Civil
Rights Act of 1964 has to do with it.

Lest you think me completely ignorant of history,
I'll admit remembering the days when the town clerk
of Barnet, Vermont, counting votes, found two
Democratic ballots and remarked, "Sumbitch voted
twice!" But I don't remember, since Puritan days in
New England, the self-righteousness that so sepa-
rates the righteous from everybody else.

This is from Bill Prince's *County News* column,
"Bill's Soapbox": "Since 1992 more than 25 people
who have been closely associated with Bill Clinton
have died. It is said they were victims of the
'Arkansas Flu'. The 'official' cause of these deaths
have been listed as everything from accidents and
plane crashes to murder and suicide. This flu bug is
more deadly than AIDS."

Terry Mattingly of the Scripps Howard News
Service, appearing in the *Tyler Morning Telegraph*,
practically salivates on the page as he describes the
discomfiture of another liberal icon: ". . . the Episco-
pal Church went into damage-control mode this
week as [Penthouse's] latest issue . . . featur[ed] news

of an alleged clergy sex ring in the Diocese of Long Island. It's the latest twist in the convoluted story of the Episcopalians and their evolving teachings on sex."

It's hard to believe—and I wasn't even aware of it till now—what tough shape the rest of the world is in, beyond the Sabine and Red rivers. Maybe that's the reason, in addition to the temperate climate here, that Mother's been asking me lately whether I couldn't stand retiring to rural Texas, to fish the rest of my life for crappies and channel cats, instead of brook trout.

In case I could, Tootie Kelly Real Estate stands ready to sell me a wooded waterfront lot on Lake Brownwood for a mere $15,000. "JUST DEPENDS ON TO WHAT EXTEND YOU WANT TO ROUGH IT. IF YOUR TRAVEL AUTO BREAKS DOWN THERE IS EVERYTHING FROM FLAT FIXERS TO FULL PLEDGE REPAIR MEN. THEN IF YOUR LOOKING TO BUY PROPERTY FOR A HOME AWAY FROM HOME WE HAVE REAL ESTATE PERSONAL IN THE AREA THAT CAN SHOW YOU AROUND."

I think I'd last about a week.

Pelican Creek

Dick, do you remember the time we went looking for the nudist camp, both of us on the same bike?

There are four of us sitting here side by side beside the creek in the milky Montana midday sun. Our hats lie on the grass behind us, our lunches between our knees before us. Far above us, little more than a black dot in the sky, an osprey hovers, wobbling in the wind on crooked wings. The sun is so bright at this altitude, and the sky so wide, it seems the day will never end.

The Pelican Valley is broad and green here, virtually treeless, a knee-deep meadow two miles across, pocked with gopher holes and rimmed on the southeast by 10,000-foot peaks. Pelican Creek meanders lazily westward across the floor of the valley, hidden down between grassy banks. It varies from only ten feet wide to more than twenty-five. No bigger than the brooks of our boyhood, it seems even tinier in this immensity of grass, mountains, and sky.

We took that old balloon-tired Rollfast you had out at your camp. You pedaled and I rode on the handlebars.

Only about three miles west of us, the busy East

Entrance road of Yellowstone Park is clogged with vehicles bumper to bumper—cars and trailers, Winnebagos, loaded motorcycles. Only three miles beyond that, the famous Fishing Bridge is lined with tourists, hanging over the railings to watch the trout in the glycerin-clear water below. It's the height of the season. But here in the valley, a little over an hour's walk from the trailhead, we have the sky and creek to ourselves.

Not entirely to ourselves. It's hard to erase from our memories the sign we read as we left the car: "Pelican Valley Bear Management Area (Day use only—No camping) Travel allowed between 9 a.m. and 7 p.m. Party of four or more recommended. Regulations are strictly enforced to reduce human disturbance of grizzly bears."

Our endorsement of this objective is wholehearted and unanimous. I scan the entire valley in all directions every minute or so in order that, should we spot a grizzly bear, we can make every effort to avoid disturbing him. Our initial effort no doubt would include pell-mell flight; but if the bear chose to pursue it—us, that is—flight would be unavailing. At any rate, that sign, as much as the hour-long walk in here, helps to explain our solitude.

We told Dick's parents we were going fishing, and left camp right after breakfast. We put our rods in a bush down by the outlet and started toward Route 20. We'd heard there was this nudist colony called "Friends of the Sun" or something, somewhere down near Erieville, and we were going to find it. We thought we knew where it was, so we didn't take any lunch.

If you took four fifteen-year-old boys and made them up to look like elderly men for Halloween—talcum powder or rubber bald heads, little pillows here and there, eyebrow pencil for wrinkles, bifocals—you'd get something that looked very much like this gang of four old friends sitting beside a brook eating sandwiches, oranges, and Snickers bars. As I look at us, reunited for the first time since 1950, I can see literally nothing important changed. The voices, the smiles, the eyes are still the same. We sit in exactly the same order we did over fifty years ago: Dick and Herb in the middle, the center of the group, with Pete and me on the ends. The conversation still bounces back and forth the way it used to—competitive, yet friendly—like a tennis ball between two old teams of regular doubles partners. Pete is still the butt of any kidding, irony, and double-entrendre; and I'm still half-in and half-out, listening and recording, unsure of my right to be included. Nothing has changed. But an invisible hand has brushed us all with the fine dust of time. We look like somebody's grandmother's furniture.

Herb is retelling the Saga of the Search for the Friends of the Sun. The search was one of those epic childhood adventures conceived in rumor, nurtured by a summer morning fantasy, and murdered by the reality of a hot July afternoon. The image of Herb and Dick, teetering along endless miles of dusty dirt roads on a broken-down old Rollfast in an illicit search for sleek, naked bodies lounging on the lawns of some hidden Shangri-La, is absolutely irresistible.

That was long ago and far away, just after the end of the Second World War, amid the green drumlins and alder-choked brooks of central New York. Often then, we sat beside crystal little rills and ate our lunches to the calling of crows in the lazy distance of summer afternoons. Finally one September, we went our inevitably separate ways. Dick and Herb went to the local high school and became scholars and football stars; from there, to Union and Colgate. Peter was sent to military school, and made it from there to Harvard and graduate school. I was sent to prep school in Massachusetts. After graduation, I spent the next nine years wandering toward an undergraduate degree at the College of Wooster in Ohio. We all went to work, in completely different fields; and now we're here together again in this beautiful, bear-haunted valley.

I'll bet we rode twenty miles, all day long. We looked everywhere. We heard there was a little sign by the road where the colony was. If there was, we never found it. And hot! Jesus, it was hot! We went all day without lunch, and then got back to Brown's store down at the end of the lake. We had about a buck between us. So we bought a couple orange sodas and sixteen Reese's peanut butter cups, and we just—I mean, we inhaled 'em!

A gust of wind, stronger than the rest, carries to our ears the gabbling of a distant flock of Canada geese, and I remember the crows of our green-pasture boyhood. A few yards in front of us, trout dimple the surface of the creek—big cutthroats, the first I've ever seen: extravagantly painted, as if by some overzealous taxidermist—and I see again in memory the bright little browns we stalked through cow-flop meadow brooks while the cicadas sang in the elm trees.

I look down the line of my three friends: Dick, conservative Republican, geologist, and coal mining engineer; Herb, ardent environmentalist and head of the Oklahoma Nature Conservancy; Pete, chemistry professor whose name conjures admiration whenever I invoke it in the company of chemistry professors. Midwesterners now, all of them. I'm the only one left in the East. We hardly could have gone in more divergent directions with our careers. The collective sum of the things we've done and the things we know must be amazing. But none of it seems as important at the moment as the things we did and learned together as boys fifty years ago on the limestone and watercress-sweet edge of Syracuse, New York. And the sense of nostalgia they give us that has brought us to this beautiful day together.

Half an hour ago I heard Peter whoop, just upstream of me. I looked up to see his baseball cap and head sticking up above the shoulder-high willows, and his long fly rod bent into a perfect parabola by the rush of a big cutthroat. He was ecstatically intent on the fish. Only a hundred feet above him, a great bald eagle hung almost motionless on the wind, watching them both. It was one of those pictures that will stay with me as long as I live, and—who knows?—perhaps beyond that.

We got back just before dark, and we were beat! We picked up the rods and walked the bicycle up the last hill to camp. Dick's father came out and asked if we'd done any good.

88

"No," we said, "we got skunked."

"Did you use up all your worms?" he asked us.

"Yessir."

"Hmm," he said. "I wonder whose these are that got left on the step."

My Boot's On Fire!

MY LEFT BOOT BURST SUDDENLY INTO flame—vigorous, bright orange, petroleum product–fueled flame. The people around me scattered helter-skelter in alarm. "I really hope," I thought to myself, "I really hope this is the low point of my day."

I should have known better than to get into such a pickle, but I'd done it, anyway. Living in New England, I'm quite accustomed to watching the weather sweep ominously across the continent toward an inevitable disaster in this otherwise quiet corner of the country. How many hundred times have we watched a warm wet front from Georgia or the Ohio Valley collide with cold air sweeping southeast from Manitoba? How often do you have to watch it to know the sequence: clouds, rain, slush, snow, cold, and clear? After fifty years, you don't have to be a rocket scientist to know what's going to happen. So I should have foreseen it. But we'd been so bludgeoned by lousy cross-country skiing conditions that winter, I figured they'd stay that way for the annual Canadian Ski Marathon in mid-February. Bad mistake.

Mother and I drove about five hours from the Connecticut Valley to the Ottawa Valley. The weather slowly worsened, the beginnings of the familiar stormy sequence. Gray skies at the start, rain on the windshield as we inched through Montreal at rush hour, and finally slippery slush on the roads for the last thirty miles to Montebello, Québec. I felt strongly that we'd be skiing all the next day on old, wet ice and new slop. So that night, while almost everyone else in the waxing room applied some form of regular ski wax, I feigned a superior prescience, and daubed on wet-weather klister, one of the stickiest substances known to humankind.

Many are the stories about the properties of klister. I don't know what it's made of, but it sticks like sin to everything—clothing, gloves, furniture. Unlike sin, however, it cannot be removed by repentance and grace. Only certain mineral solvents will do it. I sat on a school bus once, years ago, beside a young, long-haired skier. He had applied klister to his skis and was holding them carefully away from his body and the bus seat. But about halfway through the ride, he fell asleep, and his beautiful long hair, like Samson's, became his undoing, his Achilles' scalp. We helped him off the bus with his head firmly glued to his skis, and watched him shuffle very gingerly toward a first aid station in search of a pair of scissors.

But back to the near-present. To my dismay, when the shuttle bus dropped us off at the start the next morning, we emerged to five inches of new snow and falling temperatures. It was time to avoid making another mistake. I should have found some solvent and cleaned off the klister. But shivering with cold, I was eager to get started. So I just smeared a thick coat of wax over the klister and hoped for the best.

Sometimes that works. Usually it doesn't. This

time it didn't. Before long, clumps of snow literally three inches thick built up under my skis. Skiing was impossible. I tottered along the trail like a geisha on high wooden clogs, occasionally stopping to scrape off what I could. By the time I got to the end of the first ten-mile section of trail, I was pretty frustrated. I headed straight for the table where the Swix wax guys were dispensing expertise, assistance, and wax. They handed me a can of highly flammable solvent and a roll of super-absorbent paper towels. I soaked the towels with solvent and scrubbed. Nothing; the solvent couldn't even melt through the layer of ice that had built up over the klister. "Doesn't do it," I complained to the wax guy.

"Here!" he said. "Use the propane torch. That'll do it."

It did, too. The ice melted right away, and I was right behind it with the solvent. Everything was going fine, until suddenly the wad of towels caught fire with a whoosh. I leaped back, threw it on the snow, and stomped on it. That didn't work; and the klister stuck the wad of towels to my plastic boot sole. So now my boot was on fire. I danced about on one foot, shaking the burning foot madly and stomping on it, till some benevolent bystander tried to help by stomping on it also. But it stuck to his boot and tore in halves; so now there were two of us doing the flaming tarantella. People were shouting at me, "Put down the can! Put down the can!" I was splashing high-octane solvent around pretty liberally.

Then another bystander cried, "Stick 'em in the

snowbank, eh?" Obviously a Canadian. And obviously the best thing to do. It worked. Much warmer now, I finished the conversion to regular wax, swallowed a couple of cups of hot vegetable soup, three oatmeal cookies, and a handful of peanuts, and skied off to the next section of the marathon course.

The entire course of the Canadian Ski Marathon, divided into ten sections rated from "easy" to "very challenging," runs through bush and farmland for 160 kilometers (100 miles) along the Ottawa River between Lachute and Buckingham, Québec. Held annually since 1966, the two-day marathon attracts thousands of skiers, from amazingly fit athletes, called *Coureurs des Bois,* who ski the entire 160 kilometers with packs on their backs and camp out overnight at the halfway point, to pedestrian ski tourers ranging in age from four to eightyish. If there's one word that characterizes all of us here, it's probably "enthusiasm." In spite of the occasional broken bone, broken ski binding, broken pole (I came upon one friend trucking along with a fractured pole mended with duct tape and a piece of sapling), we're all here because we love the sport and really want to be here.

The organizers of the marathon (not a race) managed this year to set machined double tracks wherever possible for almost the whole length of the course, which made things a lot easier. They also managed to locate some new heart-stopping downhill plunges through the bushes that did not make things easier—especially after several hundred skiers had scraped off the fresh snow down to the ice beneath. I did a lot of three-point snowplowing, leaning heavily on my dragging pole tips, and often just took off my skis and hiked down the worst.

After that disastrous start, things ascended steadily. Mother was with me this year, so we were able to celebrate Valentine's Day together. While I skied, she and the dog (dogs are much more often welcome in New France than in New England) hit the art museum, the game farm, and the dog sled rides (where the dog was not welcome). I skied the second day with a man who turned out to be a Member of Parliament from Toronto and a very congenial gentleman (we're both Liberals) who skis at a very congenial pace. We pushed on late into Sunday afternoon, mile after mile, our conversation slowly dying away to nothing, to a weary sunset finish in a schoolyard just east of Ottawa. Parliament was in session the next day; so my friend found his car and drove home. The United States was on holiday the next day, so I limped back to the chateau and dined with Mother.

The burning foot turned out indeed to have been the low (if a bit farcical) point of the whole tour. The high point came that same day, a few hours later, when a perfectly polite Canadian voice skiing behind me said, "Sir? Excuse me. Sorry, but you appear to have something stuck to the heel of your boot. It looks rather like . . . ah, paper toweling."

Love and Rain

AFTER A YEAR AWAY, YOU FORGET. I DO, anyway. I forget how the solid granite mountains of the Adirondacks pull my eyes up much higher than I expected them to. Forget the majesty of three virgin white pines half a mile above camp, each more than six feet thick, but left to live by long-ago loggers. Forget that with every few hundred yards, or at each shift of the wind, comes the sound of falling water from a new direction.

It's about four o'clock on a November afternoon and beginning to get dusky. In a little while I'll get up and start back down the mountainside toward camp. Behind me then, a landmark we all know as The First Notch will sink below the curve of the hill. After a few hundred yards I should strike the old blazed line. I'll be using my flashlight by then, and may miss the trail, but it won't be too serious a thing if I do. Five minutes past that I'll come to Theriault's even older logging road in the valley and follow that down to the bridge just above camp.

Off to the west, in the bottom of the valley below me, I can hear the roar of the Ausable River; to the north, the rattle of Mossy Cascade; and on my fifty-year-old wool hunting hat, the drip of a cold rain. I've been up here a couple of hours, sitting on a big, rotting beech log, watching, remembering, and speculating. Watching the rain sweep across the mountains while the valley fills with fog; remembering this is what always happens when a cold front is sweeping in; and speculating that there'll be stars and a sliver of a moon by eight o'clock tonight. Looking about me in the chilly drizzle, with nothing to do but wait, I feel my mind wandering...

Seventy-five years ago this hillside was logged for the last time. The loggers took all softwood—pine, spruce, and hemlock. They peeled the hemlocks for their tanbark and piled it in neat stacks beside the logging road. It's there yet, half-covered in leaves, still waiting for the tanner who will never come. The loggers left the oaks and maples behind. These were trees that had spent their youth and adolescence reaching, stretching for the light far above them. With the shade removed, they grew massive trunks in order to sustain their height. Some of the sugar maples are four feet through at the butt and carry their heft all the way to seventy feet, where they divide into branches almost as thick. This is not a good place to be in a heavy windstorm.

In the fifty years since I started coming here, young beeches have begun to fill in the understory. The leaves of the saplings, which will hang on till April, infuse the lower air and rain with bright copper. When the wind stirs them, they rustle with the sound of a dozen deer stealing through the woods. Above the beeches, the great maples reach rough and gray to a sky the color of old, soapy bath water.

Nothing has happened here for hours, or appears to be happening now. A nuthatch runs headfirst down a dead beech stub. This means there are chick-adees around; and in half a minute, here they come, filtering through the underbrush like a band of for-agers, keeping in touch with their half-heard, comic little beeps.

A quick motion catches my eye, up high. Among the tops of the maples, a large black figure flaps and swoops out of sight: a pileated woodpecker. Some-where near my feet, a small rodent rustles unseen in the dead leaves. Almost more excitement than I can handle. My mind wanders perhaps more than it should. It's the mind of a man far closer to the end of his life than the beginning; there's more room for it to wander backward than forward. And so it does.

The trip over here yesterday followed the usual ritual. First across the old Connecticut River Warpath at Hanover. The French and Indians came raiding down the river many times. In February of 1704 they snowshoed south on the ice, right under where the bridge is now. They raided and burned Deerfield, Massachusetts, killed forty-nine colonists, and forced one hundred more to snowshoe back up the river with them, almost to Montreal. What a sight that must have been!—all those shattered, wounded families and weeping children, shuffling north across the snow. Fifty-five years after that, on October 30th of 1759, Major Robert Rogers of the Continental Army floated down the river on a makeshift raft on the last leg of a desperate escape from his raid on St. Francis. A lot of sadness has passed the spot where the new concrete bridge now stands.

Once across the Connecticut, I followed the valley

of the White River upstream, on secondary roads just for sentiment's sake. I slowed for the speed zone in Royalton and passed an innocuous sign commemorating the October 1780 Royalton Raid. The enemy then was half-different: Canadian Indians and American Tories, three hundred of them, led by a British lieutenant. They stole quietly down the First Branch of the White River, surprised the town, and burned as many houses and barns as they could. They killed several people and retreated back north with a couple of dozen captives.

Something small and quick flashes in the leaves beside a wind-felled tree about fifty feet away. I wait. A red squirrel leaps up onto the log and bounds along it, another squirrel right behind. They swirl around the upturned roots and disappear. I can't stay here too much longer. The cold and dark are both deepening.

I climbed up and over the Green Mountains at Brandon Gap. Halfway up the eastern slope of the pass, there's a turnout and parking area where tourists stop to spot moose in a headwater swamp below the road. Great granite cliffs rear up on both sides of the highway. Almost inexpressibly old—a billion and a half years—they crystallized into stone long before life appeared on earth, and were part of the original Adirondack Dome. They were the eastern shore of Proto-North America—much like modern Maine—protected by a broad undersea continental shelf. Then about 440 million years ago, the Proto-Eurasian tectonic plate, migrating westward, crashed into the edge of the continental shelf. Volcanoes erupted up and down what's now the Connecticut Valley. The sediments of the shelf crumpled like the front end of a car in a crash test and were turned into stone by the heat and pressure—stone that today lies under most of eastern New England. The minerals in them were melted, smeared, and concentrated into discrete little pockets. Almost half a billion years later, the descendants of European immigrants discovered and mined them for asbestos, talc, and a beautiful green serpentine granite. If I'm not running late, I almost always stop to salute these hoary ancients on my way up the mountain. If I'm hurried, I don't stop as I pass, but the irony is not lost on me.

I crossed the Long Trail at the summit of the gap and started downhill toward the old ironworks at Forestdale, leaving the Connecticut watershed for the St. Lawrence. A little later, driving much too fast over the rolling plain east of Lake Champlain, I could see the lights of the bridge at Chimney Point. From the bridge, the white-capped lake rolled gray as steel under a strong north wind. At the far end of the bridge, on the New York shore, lie the ruins of Fort Crown Point. Rogers' Colonial Rangers, then loyal subjects of King George II, left from here, rowing several bateaux, for the raid on St. Francis.

Only eighteen years later, the British were the colonials' enemy. Poor, bumbling General Burgoyne sailed through this narrow passage on his way to Saratoga. A few days earlier, camped along the lake, he'd issued perhaps the dumbest proclamation of his career, encouraging his Iroquois allies to attack colonists' farms and homesteads. He had no idea how much that would upset the folks of New England, or that they'd come swarming like angry bees to help the Revolutionary cause.

On the New York side of the lake, the bluff, gray granite walls of the Adirondacks stand across the road like fortifications. When you reach them, there's nowhere to go but left or right. I went right, to Port Henry, long ago a lake port smelting and shipping high-grade iron ore. The old fountain in the square is now a flower bed, and the movie theater a store. Early in the years of our marriage, Mother and I drove there once for a movie. Coming out onto the sidewalk after the show, we came upon a bunch of local bozos beating on a group of gentle hippies from a nearby summer music camp. An elderly local cop stood there watching, not raising a finger. Mother and I waded right in. I'm still impressed how much we managed to accomplish in about twenty seconds. And I'm amazed that I got away with what I told the old cop when it was all over, and the hippies safely on their way. Ah, we were full of it in those days!

After Port Henry, I putted through the defunct mining villages, with their cinder-block company houses and man-made mountains of tailings. Then the Tracy Road, right through the woods to the foot of the high peaks and the head of the south-flowing Hudson River. I turned north. A few minutes later I climbed over a col formed of glacial deposits in a deep valley, and I was back in the St. Lawrence watershed. The road dropped down off Round Mountain into the Ausable River valley. Just a few hundred yards past the bottom of the hill, the little truss bridge to camp appeared on my right. I stopped on the bridge to perform the usual ritual: lock the truck's front hubs into four-wheel drive, piss through the rail, and listen to the river for a minute or two. It was hard to imagine the noisy water running under the bridge flowing all the way to Lake Champlain, north in the lake, down the Richelieu, down the St. Lawrence past the Citadel of Québec and the islands of the lower river, and finally out past Belle Isle to meet the icebergs drifting south from Baffin Bay . . .

The chill creeps down inside my collar and between my shoulder blades. I hook my toes under a root, lean back, and perform a motionless situp for about a minute, tensing as many muscles as possible. And just then I hear more rustling. Not a mouse or a red squirrel this time; it's bigger, just out of my sight, almost in the notch.

I wait, but it doesn't move. It sounds like a deer swishing dead leaves aside, feeding on acorns or beech nuts. I stand up very slowly and begin creeping quietly toward it through the wet leaves and twigs, stopping to look at every step.

It's a good-sized doe, and she's pawing the leaves, all right. But she has her head up, looking off to my left, not feeding. Then I notice she has a grotesque growth on her back. I can't make it out, but I daren't go closer. So I raise my rifle very slowly and peer at it through the telescope.

It sprouts a pair of eyes, a black muzzle, and a set of antlers. It's her boyfriend! He's resting his chin impatiently on her withers in a most suggestive way. I have stumbled onto an intimate moment. These deer are—as my late mother-in-law used to say of her miniature poodles—"getting married."

Most of the local hunters would consider this the Mother Lode: a trophy and two weeks' camp meat, besides. Others would rejoice to fill out their licenses with a good buck. A few others would wait until procreation had been assured, and then blast him. Still fewer would with scientific detachment coolly observe the whole process and leave. None of these categories includes me. I'm embarrassed for all three of us. All I want is to get out of here. I wait till they're distracted and very slowly and deliberately back out the way I came, feeling with my feet till my calves bump against the beech log. Suddenly I'm surprised to see how dark it's gotten. I fish in my pocket for my little flashlight and begin shuffling down the hill, looking for the blazed line.

I've just spent the last half-hour looking back hundreds, millions, billions of years, and it must have put me in the mood. With the familiar trail passing under my rubber boots, my memory leaps back half a century, to the days when I was young in these mountains. How often then I was in love, and very well could have been shot myself—perhaps should have been. With a smile on my face, I very quietly follow the line of old blazes in the flashlight beam down toward the brook. The mist rising from the valley clouds my eyes, as if with tears, and I have to blink as I go.

Willem Lange is sixty-seven years old. He still has most of his hair and wits, but neither of his original knees.

A child of deaf parents, Will came to prep school in New England in 1950 as an alternative to reform school in his native New York state. During most of the time since, he has been collecting stories about the unique fea-  tures of his life in this surprisingly funny part of the world.

During a few absences from New England in the late 1950s, Will managed to earn an undergraduate degree in only nine years at the College of Wooster in Ohio. In between those widely scattered semesters, he worked variously as a ranch hand, Adirondak guide, preacher, construction labor- er, bobsled run announcer, assembly line worker, cab driver, bookkeeper, and bartender. After finally graduating in 1962, he taught high school English in northern New York for six years and filled summers as an Outward Bound instructor.

From 1968 to 1972, Will directed the Dartmouth Outward Bound Center. Since 1972, he has been a building and remodeling contractor in Hanover.

In 1981, he began writing a weekly column, "A Yankee Notebook," which appears in several New England newspa- pers. Since 1993, he has been a commentator on Vermont Public Radio. He has performed his reading of Charles Dickens's *A Christmas Carol* all over the northeastern United States, published several audiocassette tapes and books, and received an Emmy nomination for one of his commentaries on Vermont Public Television.

In 1973, Will founded the Geriatric Adventure Society, a loosely knit group of outdoor enthusiasts whose members have skied the two-hundred-mile Iditaski Marathon, climbed in Alaska, the Andes, and the Himalayas, bushwhacked on skis through northern New Hampshire, and paddled rivers north of the Arctic Circle.

He and his wife, Ida, who is the proprietor of a kitchen design business, have been married for forty-three years. They live on a dead-end dirt road in Etna, New Hampshire. They have three children and four grandchildren.